MONET

ON
LOCATION

MONET

ON
LOCATION

Denis Thomas

Regency House Publishing Ltd.

Claude Monet 67

Published in 1994 by
Regency House Publishing Limited
The Grange, Grange Yard
London SE1 3AG

Copyright © 1994 Regency House Publishing Limited

ISBN 1 85361 391 6

Printed in Italy

Picture acknowledgements

The Publishers would like to express their grati-
tude to the museums, galleries and collections
who have given permission to reproduce their
paintings.

Photographs were kindly supplied by the fol-
lowing:
Art Institute of Chicago: 52; Australian National
Gallery, Canberra: 53 bottom; The Bridgeman
Art Library, London/Giraudon, Paris: 2-3, 4-5,
6,7, 9 top, 10-11, 12, 13 top, 14 top, 23, 25, 28
top, 30-31, 33, 34-35, 36, 37 right, 40, 42, 43, 45
top, 57 bottom left, 57 bottom right, 62 top, 62
bottom, 64-65, 66, 68, 72 top, 73, 75, 78-79;
Brooklyn Museum, New York: 67 top;
Courtauld Institute Galleries, London: 38;
Fitzwilliam Museum, Cambridge: 55;
Fondation Wildenstein, Paris: 17; Kunsthalle,
Bremen: 22; Metropolitan Museum of Art, New
York: 19, 47 top, 49 top; Michael Busselle's
Photo Library: 13 bottom, 14 bottom, 51 left, 60
top, 68 bottom, 71 top, 71 bottom; Musée d'Art
et d'Histoire, Neuchâtel: 39; Musée d'Orsay,
Paris: 15, 29, 53 top; Musée Marmottan, Paris:
26-27, 41, 63 top, 77 top, 77 bottom; Musées
Nationaux, Paris: 28 bottom, 32; Museum of
Fine Arts, Boston: 44, 46, 47 bottom, 60 bottom;
Nasjonalgalleriet, Oslo: 61; National Gallery,
London: 18; National Gallery of Art,
Washington: 48, 58 left, 59 top; National
Gallery of Scotland, Edinburgh: 54; North
Carolina Museum of Art, Raleigh: 59 bottom:
Österreichische Galerie, Vienna: 51 right;
Picturepoint, London: 9 bottom, 21, 45 bottom,
49 bottom, 50, 57 top, 63 bottom, 67 bottom, 72
bottom; Roger-Viollet, Paris: 69, 70 bottom;
The St. Louis Art Museum: 37 left; Sterling and
Francine Clark Art Institute, Williamstown,
Massachusetts: 20, 24, 58 right; Sygma, London:
70 top.

Front Jacket: Background: The Bridgeman Art
Library, London.
Insert: Michael Busselle's Photo Library.

Back Jacket: Picturepoint, London.

The Boat at Giverny

CONTENTS

ABOVE
Red Boats, Argenteuil c.1875

RIGHT
Argenteuil, 1876

CHRONOLOGY

1840   Born in Paris

1845   Family move to Le Havre

1859   Sent to Paris to study at the
        Académie Suisse

1861   Military Service in Algeria

1862   Sketches with Jongkind and
        Boudin along the Normandy
        coast

1862   Returns to Paris to study at
        Charles Gleyre's Academy

1863   Paints at Chailly in the
        Fontainebleau Forest

1864   Excursions along the
        Normandy coast

1864   Paints at Honfleur

1865   Returns to Chailly.

1866   Studio in Paris. Paints
        Camille: *Woman in a Green
        Dress.*

1867   Moves to Ste-Adresse

1868   Rents a room at
        Bennecourt-en-Seine

1869   Paints at La Grenouillère
        with Renoir

1870   Marries Camille. Honeymoon
        at Trouville. July: outbreak
        of the Franco-Prussian War
        Monet flees to London 1871.
        In London as a refugee.
        Returns to Paris via Holland

1872   Works at Le Havre and
        Rouen

1873   Moves to Argenteuil on the
        Seine, builds a floating
        studio, 1874

1874   Return trip to paint in
        Holland

1875   Snow scenes in Argenteuil

1876   Begins Gare St-Lazare series.

1877   Paris, paints Gare St-Lazare

1878   Moves to Vétheuil-en-Seine

1881   Moves to Poissy, paints along
        the Normandy Coast

1882   Moves with family to
        Pourville

1883   Paints on Normandy coast,
        including Etretat.
        Rents a new home at
        Giverny

1884   Spends winter at Bordighera
        across the French border
        from Menton

1885   Works again at Etretat

1886   Three-month trip to Belle-Ile

1888   Spring visit to Antibes and
        Juan-les-Pins.
        Begins *Haystacks* series

1889   Visits Creuse Valley in
        central France

1890   Begins *Poplars* suite

1892   Begins *Rouen Cathedral*
        series

1896   Revisits Normandy. Paints at
        Dieppe, Pourville and
        Varengeville

1899   Visits London. Begins
        Thames series.

1900   Continues *Thames* series.
        Works at Vétheuil and on
        Seine series

1902   Begins *Waterlily* series

1908   Painting trip to Venice

1909   Begins waterlilies project,
        Nymphéas

1926   Dies at Giverny, aged 86

FROM NORMANDY TO PARIS

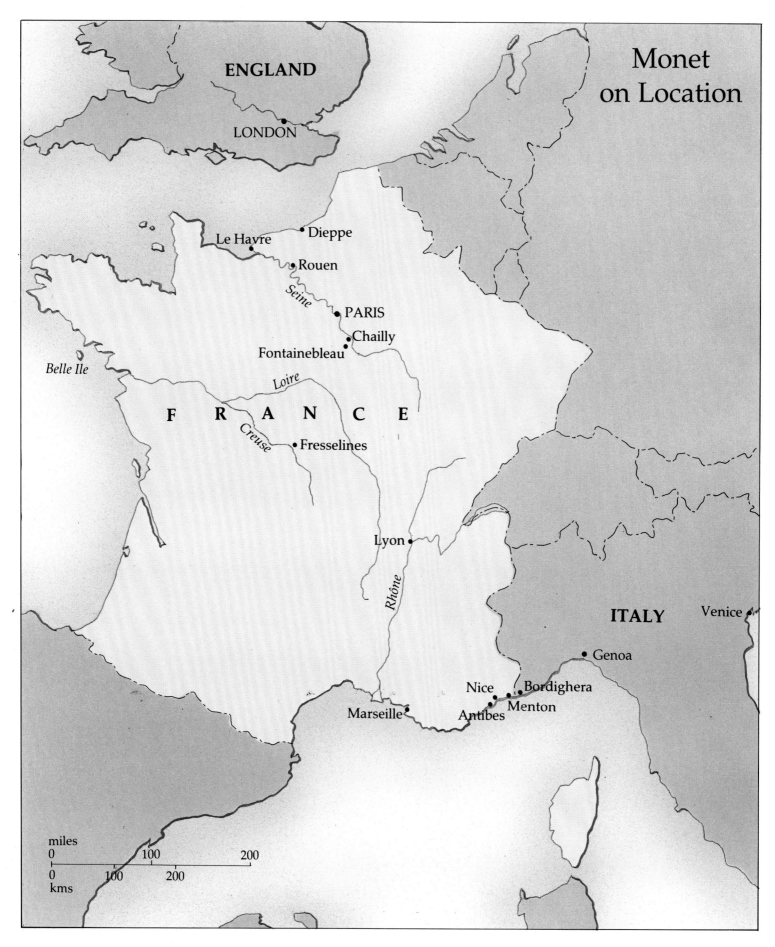

ENGLAND

LONDON

Monet
on Location

Le Havre •Dieppe

•Rouen

Seine

PARIS•
•Chailly

Fontainebleau

Belle Ile

Loire

F R A N C E

Creuse

•Fresselines

Lyon•

Rhône

ITALY   Venice•

•Genoa

Nice •
•Bordighera
Menton

Marseille•   Antibes
•

miles
0   100   200

0   100   200
kms

ABOVE
A Farmyard in Normandy, 1863

LEFT
A modern farm near Houlgate,
Normandy, France

"*As a true Parisian,*
Monet brings Paris to the
country..."

Emile Zola

Claude Monet, whose achievements have placed him among the immortals of art, admitted towards the end of his life that he was never a one for rules and regulations. There are tales of unhappy schooldays, when his teachers were liable to see caricatures of themselves in the yawning boy's exercise books. His boyhood was spent in Le Havre where he lived over his parents' grocery and ship-chandlery. Later, Emile Zola, a close friend of the group who by then had become the Impressionists' champion, was to remark that Monet had 'sucked the milk of our age'. He

NORMANDY: *a native land*

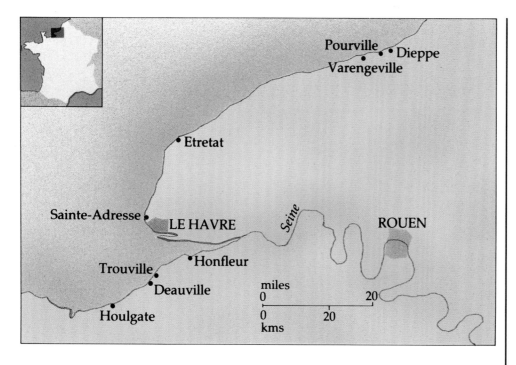

Normandy

This is where Monet's roots lay. In his early days, he roamed the coast with Boudin and Jongkind and was to return time and time again to produce some of his most powerful work. The majestic cathedral at Rouen was later to become a focus for Monet's experiments with light.

went on: 'He loves the horizons of our cities; he loves the busy people in the streets; he loves our women, their umbrellas, their gloves, their ribbons, their wigs, their face-powder, everything that makes them daughters of our civilization. As a true Parisian he brings Paris into the country.'

Early in his career he was uncommunicative about his work, and had no great faith in himself. He divided his time between Paris and the coast of Normandy, his native painting country. When he first met Eugène Boudin, who himself found all the subject-matter he needed along the coasts of Normandy, he was on the

brink of becoming a commercial artist. Born in Paris in 1840, he had spent his boyhood in Le Havre and had shown his first drawings of local scenes in the window of a neighbouring picture-framer's shop. It was there that he met Boudin, who proceeded to take him on a tour of his own local painting haunts, the beaches and pleasure resorts of Normandy. Monet's eyes were opened. He exclaimed later that it was as if a veil had been torn from his eyes.

He found Boudin's love for the place infectious. It made him realize, he said later, what painting could really mean. At the same time, appealing as they were, he did not find Boudin's subjects quite what he needed to satisfy his own ambitions. But this was not the time for hard decisions – his parents decided to send him to Paris for a formal art-school education under a renowned teacher, Thomas Couture. Monet duly arrived, presented himself, attended a few classes, then gave up. He had heard that the best place in Paris at which to study was the Académie Suisse, a less hide-bound establishment on the Quay des Orfèvres run by an ex-model who charged a fee to landscape artists anxious to improve their figure-

painting.

There he became acquainted with a tall, bearded young painter, Camille Pissarro, who turned up from time to time for life-class sessions and who was to become a life-long friend. Through Pissarro, he became familiar with the work of Corot, to which Pissarro was deeply devoted.

At this point, Monet was startled to receive call-up papers for a spell of

military service, which at that time was determined by ballot. Seven years of exile loomed ahead; but Monet seems not to have taken this misfortune too badly. He had heard from a friend that soldiering in Algeria, the invariable posting, was a rather dashing adventure. He was away for what he later called 'two delightful years' revelling in the piercing light and colourful landscape of North Africa. As things turned out, he eventually succumbed to a tropical sickness and was sent back to France for medical attention. His father, to salvage his career, decided to buy him out. Of his experiences in North Africa Monet told him: 'You cannot imagine how much I have improved my knowledge, and how much my eye has profited from it.' He wasted no time in looking up his friends, notably Boudin, who introduced him to a fellow artist, a young Dutchman destined to have a fruitful influence on Monet's career. His name was Johan Barthold Jongkind, a sketcher of great fluency and originality, who financed

ABOVE
The Beach at Sainte-Adresse, 1867

11

NORMANDY: *the early days*

his painting activities by taking odd jobs in the boatyards of Le Havre. Jongkind's obvious talent as an artist seemed to be going to waste as he traded his brilliant drawings of the local waterways and sailing craft for hard liquor.

Monet greatly admired Jongkind's crisp, animated drawings, often finished with watercolour washes, as much for their atmospheric delicacy as for their sureness of touch. To look at works by Jongkind is to marvel at a talent that has more in common with the early English masters of watercolour than with any French landscape painter of his time, ten years before the term

> *"I have painted some stunning seascapes, the regatta, and an enormous steamship."*
>
> Monet to Frédéric Bazille

BELOW
Terrace at Sainte-Adresse, 1867

TOP RIGHT
The Beach at Trouville, 1870

BELOW RIGHT
A recent view of the beach at Deauville, Normandy, France

'Impressionism' was coined. One of Monet's earliest paintings, *Beach at Sainte-Adresse,* painted in 1867, illustrates the combined influences of Boudin and Jongkind at a decisive point in Monet's career.

His father often lectured the young Claude on what was expected of him. 'Let it be understood that this time you are going to work in earnest,' he told him. 'I want to see you in a studio under the discipline of a well-known master, such as Charles Gleyre. If you choose to resume your independence I will stop your allowance.' Monet accepted this ultimatum and returned to Paris. It had been heavily hinted that he could do no better than to

emulate one of Gleyre's pupils who had lately married into the Monet family, called Toulmouche, who specialized in gracious ladies and beautiful children. Monet duly presented himself to Toulmouche in Paris, who took one look at a still-life he had set Monet to tackle and announced: 'It's good, but it's tricky. You must go to Gleyre.'

Monet failed to find a sympathetic teacher in Gleyre, despite the master's reputation. He shrank from the demands of the life-class and Gleyre's dogmatic insistence that the basis of good draughtsmanship was always

PARIS: *Renoir, Sisley and friends*

'to think of the antique'. Monet was much more in sympathy with his friends Boudin and Jongkind, footloose in a painting country they loved and which was a continuing source of inspiration to them. Another newly-arrived pupil also seemed to chafe under Gleyre's academic rigour; young Auguste Renoir. He had saved up to get to Gleyre's by putting aside some of his earnings from decorating cups and dishes with flower studies in the ornate manner of the 18th century Frenchman, François Boucher. A third new pupil now arrived on the scene; a young Englishman, Alfred Sisley, son of a businessman based in Paris. Next to join the group was Frédéric Bazille, a lanky, gentlemanly fellow from Montpellier. Monet was now reporting home that he had joined a small group of landscape painters and was working hard.

This was strictly for his parents' benefit. At Gleyre's studio he made no pretence that he was enjoying the

tuition, that he had any faith in it, or that he had any wish to be turned out like any other standard product of an art school. He considered that he was in a stronger position than his fellow students to lay down the law. Had he not gone painting with Eugène Boudin and the brilliant Jongkind? With such grounding, he did not take kindly to being treated like a novice.

The place to see how landscapes were painted, was not in a classroom but at the Louvre. It was not long before his restlessness began to infect the others. More and more he openly questioned the narrow confines of the life-class, and his ill-humour spread to other members of the group. Nevertheless, they listened to Monet. Despite his unsettled career so far, he had plenty to show for his hours of painting direct from nature. Monet's new friend, Renoir, soon became a regular copier in the Louvre, in those days an essential part of an artist's training, but not one that

ABOVE
The Seine at Rouen
BELOW
A view of Honfleur, Normandy, today
RIGHT
Women in the Garden, 1866

appealed to Monet unless he was copying landscapes. At the same time he developed an instinctive, heretical dislike of the work of the revered master draughtsman, Ingres, the great exemplar of French classical art.

PARIS: *lessons of the Louvre* _____

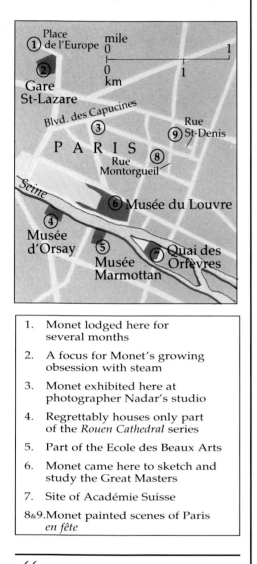

1. Monet lodged here for several months

2. A focus for Monet's growing obsession with steam

3. Monet exhibited here at photographer Nadar's studio

4. Regrettably houses only part of the *Rouen Cathedral* series

5. Part of the Ecole des Beaux Arts

6. Monet came here to sketch and study the Great Masters

7. Site of Académie Suisse

8&9. Monet painted scenes of Paris *en fête*

_____

"*He is a true master. Instead of saying Art for Art's sake he is saying Nature for Nature's sake.*"

Art Critic

_____

With the 1863 Salon exhibition looming, Gleyre, along with other prominent teachers in Paris, sounded out his pupils on the possibility of entering a work or two. The system was harsh on painters whose work was not chosen; a stencilled 'R' for 'Rejected' was stamped on the frame for all to see. That year there were more entries than ever, and a huge number – perhaps as many as 2,000 – faced rejection. To quash the inevitable protests, the Emperor, Napoleon III, decreed that all rejected works would be hung in an adjoining gallery, which was promptly dubbed 'Le Salon des Refusés'.

In the event, it proved a much bigger draw than the 'official' exhibition with its banal landscapes, complacent portraits and sanitized nudes. Parisians turned out in force to the Salon des Refusés, as if for some rare entertainment. They strolled around scoffing and laughing, encouraged by the Emperor's own example, with Manet and Whistler – both established artists – as their principal targets. Manet's sensational *Déjeuner sur l'herbe*, which the Emperor had condemned as immodest and had even struck with his cane, was to become a national *cause célèbre*.

Monet and Bazille had spent a holiday together in Chailly, on the edge of the Forest of Fontainebleau, for some outdoor sketching – though certainly not on the recommendation of Gleyre, who considered landscape painting a decaying art. Monet told his family that he discovered in the forest 'a thousand charming things' to paint and draw. The following year he rounded up an even larger group of friends, including Renoir and Sisley, whom he hoped to infect with his own enthusiasm for open-air sketching. The much-admired Barbizon painters already shared the principles which were now leading Monet and his friends in a new direction, released from the strictures of the studio. Indeed, Millet, the leading exponent of the Barbizon school, referred to 'the virgin impression of Nature'. In one of his oils from this period Monet took as his subject a party of woodcutters, in which two figures laden with fallen branches, move through a landscape of almost primal rusticity. All his friends, and notably Renoir and Sisley, began to adopt similar themes. Corot, that prince of French *plein air* artists,

advised Monet on suitable subjects and Monet accepted his advice in his *A Farmyard in Normandy*, painted in 1863. In every respect, Monet and his friends were discovering themes very far removed from the sterile classrooms of Paris.

His mind set on making his mark as a painter, Monet understood the importance of being in the centre of things. Paris was not only a unique repository of great art, but also the one and only art market that mattered. In the decade when Monet and his friends were striving to make their mark, the city was full of raw provincials such as themselves. One and all, they flocked to the Louvre, the mecca of all their hopes and aspirations.

Monet, having had his fill of copying, sought permission to set up his easel in the colonnade and pavements outside. The Louvre, in short, served more than one purpose. Not only was it the place to get acquainted with classical art, it was also a popular rendezvous, a meeting place for like-minded young artists. Monet and his friends were to become the core of what came to be known, somewhat dismissively, as *la bande à Manet* – Manet's gang – he being the prestigious flag-bearer of most of the art-related causes which Monet and his friends at that time espoused.

One of their most important causes was the idea that modern life should be portrayed as it really is and without the artificiality of academic convention imposed by previous generations. Theirs was a fast-moving age in which the railways were beginning to alter people's concept of leisure. A journey within 20 miles of Paris was no longer an expedition or a hazard. Thomas Couture, a teacher at the Ecole des Beaux Arts, urged his pupils to go on train journeys, on the grounds that they offered 'noble subjects' for a painter. Monet's fascination with the new steam age is apparent in the frequency with which he introduces trains into his paintings as well as the mighty images of such temples of steam power as the Gare Saint-Lazare.

The capital appeared, to the new generation of realists as they began to call themselves, to possess an animal energy. Only a train-fare away lay undreamed of subject-matter for a realist painter; fields and villages, waterways, winding footpaths, unexplored forests. Monet himself thought nothing of travelling from Paris to Argenteuil and back. He seems to have been the 19th century equivalent of a day-tripper, revelling in the changing scene as he revisited his native Normandy and then gradually further afield.

He was not backward, as a very young man, in presenting himself as a future candidate for fame. In Paris he contacted a professional painter, a friend of Boudin, who advised him to take care that his natural fluency did not run away with him. Monet's parents approved of any advice that would make their son knuckle down to serious study. He depended on their financial support, plus a small allowance from an aunt, to stay afloat.

His first appearance at the Salon brought him into contact with a few collectors. His own descriptions of his paintings in these early days demonstrate no false modesty. He told Bazille, who was an admittedly slow starter, that he had painted 'some stunning seascapes' during the summer of 1867, at the same time encouraging him, with characteristic worldliness, to keep up the financial assistance which he had persuaded his friend to give, and without which, he assured Bazille, he would be in a 'really awful situation'. When his lovely model, Camille, became pregnant by him, and his exasperated father refused to finance him any longer, Monet appealed to Bazille once again, adding that he was so distressed that only the other day he had 'hurled himself into the sea'. None of his friends were spared his merciless fund-raising. In April 1869 Boudin visited him and reported to a friend that Monet was 'completely starved, his wings clipped'. The two works he had submitted to the Salon had been refused and he was taking his revenge, Boudin said, by exhibiting at a Paris paint-merchant's a provocatively unorthodox study of the *Beach at Sainte-Adresse*. Boudin said: 'There is a crowd outside the window all the time. For the young people, this picture has produced fantastic

PARIS: *a glimpse of success*

reaction.'

Monet was by now becoming acquainted with the Seine estuary, two views of which he showed at the next Salon. As works were hung alphabetically, he found himself shoulder-to-shoulder with Manet, who was startled to receive congratulations on a pair of sea-pieces by Monet which hung alongside. Manet was not amused by this mistake, and swept out. The painters themselves could hardly be blamed for a mix-up in their names. Their subject-matter and painterly styles were quite different even though Monet had once, to his surprise, been complimented in the press for the excellence of a work by the already-celebrated Manet.

Long before his career began to take shape, in the days when he was starting to re-acquaint himself with his native Normandy, Monet had explored the dramatic coastline of Etretat, between Dieppe and Le Havre – a wild, gaunt stretch stimulating enough to have fired the imaginations not only of his writer friend Guy de Maupassant, but also of the painters Courbet and Boudin.

In the spring of 1864 he left Paris for Honfleur, to look for subjects on his own home ground. He wrote to Bazille that he was getting up at five o'clock in the morning and discovering more and more beautiful things to paint: 'I have such a desire to do everything, my head is bursting

with it.' He asked Bazille to join him on a painting jaunt to the Forest of Fontainebleau. Two marine subjects exhibited by Monet in the Salon of 1865 were well received. The *Gazette des Beaux Arts* wrote of them in complimentary terms: 'The striking viewpoint, the bold way of looking at things, of compelling the viewer's attention, are qualities which M.

ABOVE
Bathers at La Grenouillère, 1869

RIGHT
La Grenouillère, 1869

Monet already possesses in a high degree. His *Mouth of the Seine at Honfleur* stopped us in our tracks and we shall not forget it.' Bazille reported to his parents that Monet had had a much greater success than he had expected. Emile Zola, ever ready to support his friends, wrote enthusiastically of Monet's *Road in the Forest of Fontainebleau*. Monet was promptly welcomed to the ranks of the 'naturalists', as the group were then called. He would have been well aware that most of these reviewers were champions of Manet, the acknowledged leader of the avant-garde; but every word of encouragement counted.

Any news of his son's progress was welcome to Monet's father, who had agonized over his prospects ever since rescuing him from his National Service. Other signs of acknowledgement were beginning to surface. An article in the professional journal *Artiste*, would have also helped reinforce Monet's growing respectability as an artist. A new young school of painting, inspired by Courbet, was beginning to cause a stir in the art world. Monet's own definition of his aims began to be more comprehensive: 'The expression of life on all levels, its sole aim to represent Nature. It is truth balanced with science, embracing all the forms of the

visible world.'

These enthusiastic claims, laudable though they may have been, were not at once adopted by the young artists concerned. Monet persisted with his explorations of light and colour, and in the summer of 1866 decided to paint his first large out-of-doors picture. This was *Women in the Garden*, set in Corot's favourite painting country near St-Cloud. Courbet arrived to see how Monet was progressing and found him idling because, as he said, the sun had gone in. Courbet urged him to work on the background while waiting for the sun to reappear. Monet was unimpressed with this idea; he insisted that in order

FROM PARIS TO THE SEINE

to preserve the integrity of an open-air picture once it had been begun, it was essential to wait for an approximation of the original conditions to reappear before continuing. Otherwise he might just as well paint the entire thing in his own studio. The sun eventually reappeared; Monet picked up his brush; and the result is one of the most successful and inspiring works of his early years.

Perhaps the most impressive of these large *al fresco* works is his *Terrace at Sainte-Adresse,* for which Monet posed his father in the foreground admiring a distant view of shipping, and used small brush-

"I'm so happy here, surrounded by all that I love. I paint on the shingle when the weather is stormy or when the boats go out fishing. I find it more agreeable here in winter than in summer"
Monet, writing from Etretat

strokes to achieve an effect of flickering seaside light. Unfortunately for Monet, these works on a grand scale did nothing to help him keep afloat financially. Sorely pressed for cash and concerned for Camille, he appealed to the ever-loyal Bazille, who generously agreed to buy *Women in the Garden.* They settled on a price of 2,500 francs to be paid in monthly instalments of 50 francs – a commitment that would prove very difficult to honour. Monet struggled on. He appealed to his father for help to be told that he was welcome to bed and board in the family home, but that funding was out of the question.

Monet continued to scrape along. Camille waited for her baby in Paris. Monet's *Women in the Garden* was rejected by the Salon in 1867; it is now in the Louvre.

His friends were in no easier plight. Frozen out by the Parisian art establishment, they drew up a petition for a regular Salon des Refusés, though with scant expectation that it would be granted. Their friend Zola did what he could by writing derogatory reviews in the press ridiculing mainstream art. Monet moved into his aunt's house at Sainte-Adresse and managed to keep his output going – 20 on the way, he announced, some stunning marines, some figures, gardens, the regatta at Le Havre, an enormous steamship. Some of this new work descended on the faithful Bazille – he already had Sisley and the penniless Renoir under his roof – and Monet painted a picture of Camille with their newly-arrived son Jean.

At an exhibition of marine painting at Le Havre he, Manet and Courbet were all awarded silver medals but sold not a single painting between them. Some of the group persisted with the Salon, with only marginal success. Again Monet was obliged to dump his sorrows in Bazille's lap. He had just been thrown out of an inn, he wrote, and stark naked at that. His family had no intention of doing any more for him. He dreamed of a better life, a cosy little family in a cottage with a good fire.

A sunnier side of Monet emerges in the paintings he made, often in the company of Renoir, along the Seine in 1869. Monet, Camille and little Jean were living at Bougival, north-west of Paris. His friend Renoir had persuaded his parents to take him back, and they found room for him in their home at Ville d'Avray. The right bank of the Seine at that time was fast becoming a pleasure-ground. With the suburbs of Paris creeping ever nearer, it was easily accessible for day-trips or boating jaunts, while retaining a pleasingly rustic character. The lively bars and cafés, and the novelty of

boat trips along the Seine, appealed strongly to the young painters on their outings. At Argenteuil, Monet was struck by the animation of a scene that summed up the new realism: the vibrance of ordinary people having fun, the transparency and shimmer of fresh air and water.

Monet's mentor, Boudin, had amply shown him the great advantage of painting on the spot and the sense of immediacy it can bring to the image, a thing rather more difficult to capture in the studio. It appealed to Monet as a method that dispensed with academic conventions and time-honoured notions of composition with no loss of painterly quality. Paintings,

LEFT
The Cliffs at Etretat, 1885

BELOW
A view of present day Etretat, Normandy

they found, would 'work' even on thinly prepared surfaces, which added luminosity and a sense of movement. When working outside, Monet and his friends took their own studio light with them.

Monet, through his contact with Boudin early on, had become more and more aware of the limitations of studio painting. He may not have reached this conclusion intellectually, but it lay at the heart of what was soon to become known as 'Impressionism'.

In historical terms its beginnings date from 1869, when Monet and Renoir first discovered La Grenouillère (The Frogpool) on the banks of the Seine. There were two such resorts in the vicinity of Bougival, both within easy distance of Paris by rail. La Grenouillère was listed in the travel guides of the time as an entertaining place to eat, swim or go boating. The establishment was tethered to the river

ALONG THE SEINE

LEFT
Woman in a Green Dress
(Camille), 1866

ABOVE
Fisherman's Cottage on the Cliffs at
Varengeville, 1882

bank, and access was by duckboards which were apt to submerge if patrons were caught in a swell. It had a somewhat raffish reputation as the Moulin de la Galette of the suburbs. There is a passage in one of Maupassant's novels, *La Femme de Paul,* which could be applied to this popular venue: 'a haunt of distinguished riff-raff, ham actors and lowly journalists'. Whatever its reputation, it could never have been expected that it would be later immortalized in paint.

The style that Monet had first developed while painting with Boudin now became part of his method. Even a shadow, Monet noted, can be made up of light. Side by side at the river's edge, painting the scene of bohemian life, he and Renoir must have wondered at the direction their careers were taking. Meanwhile, there was little change in Monet's financial situation. Both his latest Salon entries had been turned down. As he told Bazille – no sales; only a silver medal worth 15 francs, some reviews in local papers, a study of Camille as the *Woman in a Green Dress.* His creditors had seized all his other paintings which they proceeded to sell off at 80 francs apiece.

In the summer of 1870, Monet was just 30. He and Camille, newly married and with little Jean, were at Trouville with Camille's sister, enjoying a break on the Normandy beaches. There Monet, holding a canvas on his knee, painted the two young women, their parasols shading them from the bright sun. Within a few days everything had changed – the Prussians were marching on Paris. Plans and ambitions for the future were swept aside. After some hesitation Monet decided that the family would have to split up and that he would get away to England. In August, Bazille enlisted in a unit of the Zouaves – a patriotic gesture typical of his family tradition and breeding. After some delays, Monet

A REFUGEE IN LONDON

managed to reach London and began to seek out fellow refugees. A few weeks later France was overwhelmed, Bazille lay dead, and Paris was under occupation.

It did not take Monet long to get his bearings on the other side of the Channel. A widely-known landscape painter whom French artists of Monet's generation held in regard, Charles-François Daubigny, had already arrived. It was he who, in a typical art-world wrangle in Paris, had protested against the Salon's refusal to admit a single work of Monet's and

had resigned in protest. Daubigny's own reputation in Paris was suffering as a result of his having supported the 'wrong' side of the argument. His honourable intentions had done his official status no good at all. Daubigny was a leading member of the Barbizon School, whose attitudes and beliefs had inspired Monet in his early days. Like others of his group, he believed in getting inside the environment. He preferred to work in close proximity to ordinary people, getting as near to their way of life and work as possible. Daubigny and his

friends had a natural aversion to the ponderous machinations of the art world, and to the dictates of popular taste. They were attempting through their art to establish a peaceful social and moral revolution. They wanted nothing to do with the allegories and images of history and mythology, but

BELOW
Tulip Fields at Sassenheim, near Leyden, 1886

RIGHT
Port de Zaandam, 1871

aimed to record at first hand the values and experiences of the everyday world. Though revolutionaries at heart, their goal was to achieve a new concept of communication and harmony with Nature. In their down-to-earth way Daubigny and his friends were just as determined to succeed in their aims as was the rather more aggressively obstinate Monet.

In London, Daubigny had met the Paris dealer, Paul Durand-Ruel. More than any other single individual, he was to develop a market for what became Impressionist art. He was already acquainted with Manet and his circle and was attempting to interest dealers in their work; so far without any great success. He had lately opened a gallery in New Bond Street, in the hopes of showing contemporary French painting there. Though he was prepared to wait, he was somewhat depressed at the

general lack of enthusiasm in London for unfamiliar art of any kind.

Before long Monet was delighted to find a fellow exile, in the person of Camille Pissarro, also taking refuge in London. Pissarro, who had been obliged to leave his home in Louveciennes in the face of the invaders, had been forced to virtually leave his life's work behind. Since his arrival, he had become attracted to the sights of suburban London. 'While Monet worked in the parks,' he wrote later, 'I was in Lower Norwood studying the effects of fog and snow. We also visited the museums. We admired Gainsborough, Lawrence and Reynolds. But we were struck chiefly by the landscape painters, who shared our aim with regard to the open air, light and fugitive effects.' He delighted in such ordinary scenes as Penge Railway Station, which he painted, and more celebrated sights such as the Crystal Palace.

Monet's response to London was broader than Pissarro's. He sketched in the parks, and even submitted a couple of works to the Royal Academy...'though naturally,' he said later, 'they were turned down.' Both exiles were to become familiar with the Constables and Turners in the National Collection. For all their own sturdy nationalism, they regarded them with respect and admiration.

Monet's new contact, Durand-Ruel, was one of those dealers, uncommon at the time, who combine a good eye for a picture with a talent for getting along well with artists. 'A genuine picture dealer,' he declared, 'ought to be at the same time an intelligent connoisseur, ready if need be to sacrifice what seems to be his immediate interests to his artistic convictions. He should prefer to fight speculators rather than join in their activities.' Over the next five years he was to organize ten exhibitions in

THE SEINE: *the aftermath of war* _____

London, showing works by Monet and Sisley, Pissarro, Renoir and Degas. In supporting Monet and his friends he alienated the Salon artists, most of whom held the newcomers in disdain. Like the self-exiled Pissarro and Monet, he returned to Paris to find the economy wrecked, like so much else in France, by the war and its bloody aftermath, the Commune. To meet his bills he was obliged to sell works by such established painters as Corot, Delacroix, Millet and Rousseau. At the height of the depression he began buying works by Monet at the then respectable price of 300 francs.

Monet had returned to France via Holland, where he paused to paint such traditional scenes as whirring windmills beneath huge skies and narrow canals with houses seemingly growing straight out of the water. Pissarro, who had been informed that the Prussians had taken over his home as a billet, found on his return that the paintings he had left behind had been used as duckboards. The unquenchable Emile Zola was issuing a call for recovery: 'This is the time for a few home truths. After any disaster there follows a certain stupor, a desire to return to unsullied reality. We look around for firmer ground to build on. All great literary and artistic blossomings have taken place in times of either complete maturity or violent upheaval. I hope that, from all this expense of blood and this stupidity there will emerge a stronger tide, and that those who were lately regarded as pariahs' (he meant Monet and company, along with Boudin) 'will now come to the fore.'

Monet's first call was on Courbet, who had been cruelly treated as an 'enemy of the Republic', imprisoned, and only released on medical grounds. Soon Monet was calling on Paul Durand-Ruel and urging support for that group of artists most in need, himself included. Durand-Ruel responded by buying several works from them, as well as a large number from Manet's studio. He then assembled the first joint exhibition of the friends' work to show in his gallery. There were thirteen Manets,

nine by Pissarro, six by Sisley, four by Monet and three by Degas – an impressive example of moral support. Because Durand-Ruel had his hands on so many of their works, very few of the group submitted paintings to the Salon that year.

LEFT
Impression: Sunrise, 1872

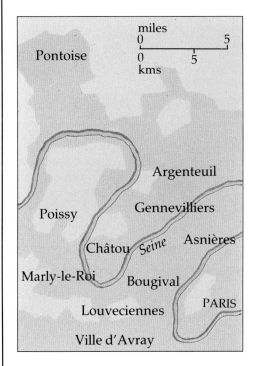

The Cradle of Impressionism

With the development of the railway, the outskirts of Paris and the towns along the Seine were becoming more accessible to Monet and his friends who made painting trips to such pleasure resorts as La Grenouillère. Monet and his family went to live at several locations, among them Argenteuil, Vétheuil, Bougival and Poissy in a natural progression towards Giverny, Monet's last resting place

A HOME BY THE RIVER

Monet, reunited with Camille and little Jean – they had spent the war *chez* Boudin – rented a small house at Argenteuil, on the banks of the Seine, where as if to celebrate his reunion with his young family, Monet plunged happily into a round of sketching. The quality of this outpouring – river scenes in particular, including *Yacht Races at Argenteuil* and *The Bridge at Argenteuil*, both now in the Louvre – was never surpassed. He painted the Seine in its sunniest moods, vibrant with light; broad, bright sweeps of the brush; reflections redoubling the vivacity of the subject with a spontaneity and harmony of design.

Renoir, as an old friend, always arrived with paints and easel. Argenteuil was then an attractive place, just far enough from the city to maintain its tranquillity, yet within easy reach of the bustle of the art world. Monet may have chosen it on the recommendation of Manet, whose family for some years lived on the other side of the river. Monet would have found it particularly attractive as a centre for sailing. Ever alert to open-air pastimes, he was extremely fond of boating, both for outings and as a spectacle. He belonged to the category of painters, dubbed by Zola *Les*

ABOVE LEFT
Railway Bridge near Argenteuil, 1874 (detail)

LEFT
Yacht Races at Argenteuil, 1872

ABOVE
The Bridge at Argenteuil, c. 1874

Actualitistes – those who try above all to penetrate to the very essence of things. Zola considered that their works were alive because they were taken from life itself, and painted with a love of the contemporary world as they saw it.

PARIS: *the first manifesto* _____

The Regatta at Sainte-Adresse, 1867

Monet's paintings of life along the Seine are a good example of this. His six years at Argenteuil produced some 170 works, varying from scenes around the town to views from the surrounding hills, as in *A Path through the Vineyards,* which shows not too-distant industrial chimneys, smoking away in peaceful co-existence with the countryside.

He was fortunate in discovering a wealth of human activity on his own doorstep. He might have expected to become a local celebrity, or at least a 'character'; but apparently not. He remained an outsider, going his own way, largely ignored or unnoticed. The fact that he sent his son to the local school did not make the Monets, in local terms, members of the community.

Nor do these times appear to have been prosperous for Monet. He wrote to Manet in June 1875 asking if he could spare a 20-franc note by return of post; and to Georges de Bellio, who had bought a couple of sketches from him, pleading that he and his family were going to be turned out of 'this dear little house where I have led such a simple life and am able to work so well,' adding, 'I do not know what will become of us. Yet I had so much fire in me and so many plans.'

It was hardly a year since Monet and his friends had arranged an exhibition in the studio of a friend of theirs, the photographer Nadar, in the Boulevard des Capucines in Paris. Thirty artists put their names to a manifesto issued by a self-styled co-operative, the *Société Anonyme Coopérative d'Artistes-Peintres -Sculpteurs, -Graveurs.* The artists involved, including Monet, had from time to time had works accepted at the annual Salon.

Monet had been successful only once, in 1868. In the following two years his entries were rejected. He and his friends, who had shared the same experience, decided that it was time to bring their work to public notice regardless of convention and policy, perhaps even of the law.

They were not an organized group. They had no coherent cause

Birth of the Impressionists

or manifesto to bring before the public, simply their work, as yet unknown, under their largely unrecognised names. Most were hard up, a few claimed to be starving, others scratched a living on the fringes of commercial art.

The group now included one woman, Berthe Morisot, and one relatively well-known painter, Monet's friend and mentor, Eugène Boudin. Monet's exhibits included a vivid sketch of a sea-mist with the title *Impression: Sunrise.* He had painted it at Le Havre in the spring of 1872, a sketch to catch a light effect that dissolved almost in the instant that he set it down.

The title he gave it was as spontaneous as the subject which had

presented itself was unexpected. The critic Louis Leroy is credited with using the term 'impression', though in a derogatory sense, in his review for the journal *Charivari.* His article took the form of an imaginary visit by a respectable landscape painter who is sent into shock at the sight of so many deranged images in one place at one time.

The label 'Impressionist' stuck. Renoir was one of the first to embrace the name. He maintained that it would give the public an idea of what to expect of the group in the future. It says: 'Here is the kind of painting you won't like – if you come back.' Monet and his colleagues accepted the term as a compliment. It did not fully describe their objectives but it would

serve as a rough-and-ready identity for a dozen or so young men and women who had been swept up together in the quest for a new modernism that reflected the changing times. They took half-a-dozen of their predecessors into their embrace, notably Delacroix, Corot and Courbet. In the opinion of the friends, the accepted view of art and taste as

ABOVE
Landscape View of the Plain of Argenteuil, 1872

RIGHT
Woman with a Parasol – Madame Monet and Her Son, 1875

accepted by the Establishment of their times was synonymous with mediocrity.

As the doyen of art historians, John Rewald, has pointed out – the term 'Impressionism', coined in derision, was soon accepted by the painters themselves. Charged with ridicule, and vague though it was, Impressionism seemed as good a term as any to underline the common element in their work. Its true meaning would come to be understood in the work of the painters themselves in the way they strove to capture the sense or experience of the subject rather than to record it in precise detail. They selected one element – light – to interpret all of Nature. Contradictions between one early example and another do not invalidate the painters' aims. Monet, within a couple of years, would turn towards an unashamedly decorative mode in two studies of a *Woman with a Parasol*, the figures standing on a grassy knoll against a windy sky.

The drama of the first Impressionist exhibition did much to keep alive a legend that had done so much to win sympathy for a courageous group of friends, some touched with genius, at a critical moment in their careers. But no historic event can be entirely accidental. Factors unrecognized at the time may well precipitate future events. The emergence of the Impressionists must be seen in the context of their times. The strength of public feeling in France and the general reaction to the disgrace of 1870 and nationwide collapse of morale, continued to gnaw away at the French's sense of patriotism.

The loss of territory, and the humiliating terms of surrender, had left the populace in a state of demoralization. To recapture its pre-war belief in itself, as reflected in its achievements in the arts under the Empire, became a national concern. The priority now, so soon after France's greatest humiliation of modern times, was a return to high-mindedness, morality and patriotism, in all of which the arts could be seen as having a pivotal role to play.

As an example, the newly-appointed Director of Fine Arts had welcomed the Salon of 1872 as a chance to show 'jealous Europe' what the genius of France could still produce in the aftermath of its defeat. The Salon that year did not rise to the occasion. Art, with the strong feelings it traditionally arouses, was in limbo. Then along came this group of revolutionaries, the Impressionists as they were shamelessly called, apparently playing the fool in public in the name of art. Monet's *Impression: Sunrise* was seen as an act of provocation. 'Seeing the lot,' wrote *La Patrie*, 'you burst out laughing. But with the last ones you finally get angry.'

Though Monet had neither been in France during the war nor suffered the atrocities of the Commune, he had nevertheless expressed concern about the situation. He would have experienced pangs of dismay when travelling back to Paris across a countryside that had only recently been evacuated by the enemy, to find that reports of wholesale destruction had been true. Similar misgivings must have struck him when he left

SCENES ALONG THE SEINE _____

Train in the Countryside, 1870

Paris to settle in Argenteuil, barely 11 km from the capital. It had been occupied by the Prussians and had lost its railway and road bridges, the latter having been burned by the French themselves as they retreated.

However, when Monet painted the road bridge soon after arriving at Argenteuil, it is seen as rebuilt and already open to traffic. He painted many such pictures as he settled in, among them *The Bridge at Argenteuil Under Repair* and *Train and Factories at Robec*. Not since the industrial landscapes executed in the first years of his career had Monet been so conscious of the twin themes of industry and progress. In 1872, the year of his return, Monet earned more than 12,000 francs. These images of regeneration suggest a growing sense of hope in the future. *Impression: Sunrise* might also be seen in this context. It shows a scene guaranteed to raise the spirits and rekindle feelings of patriotism.

Of Monet's exhibits in the following year's show no fewer than twelve were pastels, listed simply as 'sketches'. He had learned this elusive craft from Boudin, probably on their early outings together. Boudin had a great love of the medium and had accumulated several hundred during his years of sketching along the shores and waterfronts of Normandy, recording cloud effects for possible use in paintings, sometimes in sequence hour by hour.

In Monet's hands, pastel assumed the delicacy of watercolour, a technique he admired in the work of the other friend of his early days, Jongkind, and which he seems to have used, somewhat cautiously, in conjunction with pastel. Other such studies include paintings in oils on panels, an outdoor technique which was developed by *plein air* masters of the 1840s.

His interest in the effects of light on woodland had been inherited from the Barbizon painters. He simplified its effect on trees by broadening his brush strokes and dramatizing places where the sun's rays fell unimpeded. As a pupil at Gleyre's Academy, he had discovered Fontainebleau and its undisturbed forest; a theme he returned to again and again.

One of his early views of the surrounding countryside, *Landscape View of the Plain of Argenteuil*, reveals an almost classical landscape. This approach is rather unusual for Monet in its apparent return to an earlier tradition of French landscape painting. The subject is treated reverentially, in a somewhat devotional mood rather more often seen in the work of the less sophisticated Pissarro.

A more typically Impressionist impulse can be seen in Monet's *Train in the Countryside* (left) painted as early as 1870, in which figures with parasols are seen strolling under a sunny sky while on an embankment high up behind them, half-screened by trees, a line of box-like coaches dotted with figures trails a plume of decorative smoke. It is the kind of subject that the art establishment of the time might have seen as directly opposed to France's tradition of landscape painting.

What has been dubbed 'the cradle of Impressionism' is centred to the north-west of Paris and embraces the suburban villages of Argenteuil, Bougival, Louveciennes, and Marly-le-Roi. These place names and half-a-dozen others embrace an area which is synonymous with the development of Impressionism. Monet had settled with Camille at Bougival in 1869. It was a location already familiar to the Barbizon painters, who had worked around Fontainebleau in the 1860s. The area was recognized as an artist's colony long before Monet became aware of it.

Renoir credited Monet with doing all he could to encourage other members of the group. It was he who opened their eyes, Renoir said later, to the necessity of adopting methods which were to safeguard the art business. 'We know that railways have supplanted stage-coaches,' said Monet, 'as a means of travel. No one nowadays would think of going to Lyon in a stage-coach because there are no longer any. Then why should painters seek their livelihood

BELLE-ILE: *the primacy of light*

courting this or that rich patron, since there are no rich patrons left? What do we get from them anyway? Only a miserable portrait from time to time, and after living for a week on the proceeds we are as hard up as ever. Just as we can go by rail,' he went on, 'using the cushioned seats and palatial stations which are paid for by the

ABOVE
Storm: Rocks at Belle-Ile, 1886

RIGHT
Rocky Headland at Belle-Ile, 1886

FAR RIGHT
The Rocks at Belle-Ile, 1886

huge number of travellers, so we painters ought to sell our work to dealers, whose luxurious galleries will be paid for by hundreds of customers. The day of the little individual merchant, and of personal bartering, is over. We have entered the era of Big Business. While our dealers are busy attracting customers, we shall be able to do our painting far away from Paris – in China, Africa, or any place where we find subjects which inspire and please us.'

These prophecies, as Renoir observed, were a waste of breath. Such a system was already under way, and Durand-Ruel was the man to turn it into an entirely new profession. Had

they but known it, he was to secure for his painters an artistic lustre unequalled since the Renaissance.

To the original group, headed by Monet, the problem was how to get their point of view over to the public. To describe what the Impressionists were striving to achieve was somewhat elusive and difficult to describe in concrete terms, a fact guaranteed to confuse the spectator and irritate the critic.

There were no rules or standards on offer by which the end result could be judged. Every painter was entitled to make up his own rules. The quality of the paint, the whole apparatus of creating a picture, played its part in the whole.

In a typical Monet, light is everywhere; even in the shadows. The Impressionist idea of shade is simply a complementary tone which includes the surrounding primary colours. The sense of light is all-pervading. The brushwork consists of small dabs of colour which, in juxtaposition, suggest form. Though easy enough to recognize, all this nevertheless demanded effort from both the painter and the viewer. It was all too much for the Salon – a disappointment with which Monet was forced to come to terms. He and Renoir, old painting companions of the 1860s, had completed a process

---

"The sea here is giving me a terrible time. It is so unlike the sea I am used to painting"

Claude Monet

---

which had begun a dozen years before, when their respected senior member, Edouard Manet, had drawn crowds to the Salon des Refusés with his *Déjeuner sur l'herbe*.

Each little rustic township along the Seine had its own unique atmosphere. At one time or another practically all the members of the group had worked in the locality, headed by Monet, Renoir and Manet. Monet was having his usual difficulties with landlords, and it was Manet who came to his rescue by helping to find a house for him at Argenteuil. Manet himself was attracted to the opposite side of the river, to Gennevilliers, where his

family owned a property.

For Manet it was a decisive experience. It convinced him, once and for all, that the true environment for painting, as Monet kept insisting, was out-of-doors rather than in the studio. In his garden at Argenteuil, Monet began to paint family groups, visitors, and other members of the circle, in outdoor settings of the kind that had attracted Bazille before the war. Manet's subjects included Camille with her young son under a tree and Monet entering from the left. Renoir turned up, joined them, and set to work with borrowed paints and brushes. When he had finished his picture he presented it to Monet. The episode, well documented, seems to mark a high point in the group's affection for one another. Monet had a special place for the picture among the jumble of his friends' work

THE SEINE: *afloat at Argenteuil*

which he held on to for the rest of his life.

Monet's first major attempt in 1866 at working outdoors on a large canvas, *Women in the Garden,* had not been repeated. When, in the 1880s, he decided to send again to the official Salon, he submitted works that he had enlarged in the studio from smaller paintings done out-of-doors. His landscapes shown in the first Impressionist exhibition were mostly small works painted outside.

However, the experience of working direct from nature revealed the limitations, as well as the potential, of the method. Sensitivity to minute changes of light made it almost impossible to record quickly enough what he saw before everything shifted. He realized that making a picture – a

ABOVE
The Seine at Argenteuil, Autumn, 1873

RIGHT
The Studio Boat at Argenteuil, c.1874

" *Everything is gaiety, clarity, joyous countryside, rivers crowded with pleasure-boats, the life of outdoors, forever charming* "
Armand Silvestre

---

two-dimensional coloured surface – imposed different demands from simply recording natural effects. Monet's work method shows a tendency to modify his open-air approach by retouching his outdoor subjects in the studio. He seems to have persisted in this method: he wrote to Durand-Ruel insisting that his latest painting, *Rocky Headland at Belle-Ile,* needed to be worked over in peace and quiet.

Durand-Ruel was not short of comment on his client's subject-matter. His friend Armand Silvestre told him: 'Monet loves to juxtapose on the lightly ruffled surface of water the multi-coloured reflections of the setting sun, brightly coloured boats, changing clouds. His view of the shore is vague, the houses broken down as if in children's games, objects assembled from odd pieces. His tonal range is extraordinarily bright – everything is gaiety, clarity, joyous countryside, rivers crowded with pleasure-boats, skies that shine with light mists – the life of the outdoors, forever charming.'

When Monet temporarily deserted Durand-Ruel to help a rival dealer launch a new gallery in Paris, he was publicized as quite a catch. An article in the *Gazette des Beaux Arts* acknowledged that he was a member of the Impressionist brotherhood, adding: 'Any painter who lays claim to absolute realism must wonder why popular acclaim eludes him,' and quoted as an example one of his recent paintings – 'a mighty cliff, its twisted vegetation seared by the sea air, contemplating the silhouette of its shadow in the blue water.' Monet was by now the acknowledged successor to Corot and Courbet. He had done away with the traditional clutter of first thoughts, second thoughts, cancellations, revisions – the whole process which was generally

considered essential in making a picture – and had virtually turned his back on working in a studio. The critics were now becoming familiar with his method, one that contradicted all academic practices.

Comparison of much Impressionist work from the 1870s with previous French landscape painting shows a very different use of colour in the structure of the picture. In *The Seine at Argenteuil, Autumn*, 1873, Monet models the scene by means of colour changes. Soft blues and greens set off the vivid yellows and oranges of the sunlight, rather than using dark and light tones for shadows and highlights. This modelling by colour Pissarro had taught Cézanne as the basis of their new method in the 1870s. At first it was only in sunlit scenes that clear contrasting colour was used. The move towards colour-modelling was the result of perceiving nature in terms of colour rather than of tone. In the mid-1880s, Monet and Renoir keyed up their colour still further, mixing their paints with white to heighten the luminosity of the scene.

This technique would also be used by Monet and by Renoir to capture the brightness and dazzle of the Mediterranean.

To an artist who took genuine pleasure in landscape painting, Argenteuil might have seemed somewhat fickle in its variations of light, haze and mists. Monet was enough of a realist not to expect too much stimulation in suburban life or to resent the signs of creeping urbanization all around him. He had only to turn his head in the opposite direction to be rewarded with swaying leaves and a looping towpath that invited him to carry his paints and canvas with him. Argenteuil was to Monet as good a place as any to pursue his career as a realist painter, and at the same time discover for himself the most fruitful way forward. There is tenderness in his treatment of fields and lanes veiled in misty gloom; unremarkable homesteads with gardens full of vegetables; workaday sheds and trellis fences. He was no less stimulated in mid-winter as in the summer months – there are numerous studies of trodden snow as winter closed in. He turned out in a snowstorm to paint the newly-arrived steam train from Paris, its lamps dim with snow and its smoke-stack belching into the pallid air.

His colour sense was growing more and more expressive, his subjects in all ways sympathetic. Among the most beguiling works which we owe to Argenteuil are those of, or painted from, his floating studio, a contraption consisting of a rowing boat rigged up with a lightweight roof, with supporting struts to hold an easel and canvas. From this floating studio Monet enjoyed painting himself and Camille afloat. He became quite adventurous: by installing primitive sleeping quarters he was able to take Camille on lengthy excursions, on one occasion all the way to Rouen. Through these river trips Monet made a valuable new friend, Gustave Caillebotte, a shipwright and engineer, owner of several river craft and himself an accomplished painter. He

PARIS: *under the hammer*

is remembered to this day for bequeathing his superb collection of early Impressionist paintings to the Louvre, the historic bequest that bears his name. His first acquisitions, inevitably, were works by Monet and Renoir. The little group found their most pleasurable subjects in these friendly waters; but sales were hard to come by. Of the friends, Renoir was now having more success than the others, his subjects being mainly portraits and nudes. Renoir's personality, cheerful and easy-going, helped him to make friends with his clients, including several who had no time for Impressionism in general. Durand-Ruel, with heavy stocks in his gallery, could only urge Monet to be patient: his time would come.

Meanwhile, life was becoming more and more expensive. Prices were rising, headed by rents and food. New taxes to help pay off the crippling reparations debt to the Prussians hurt everybody, rich or poor. Nobody was spared. In the art market practically the only works to find buyers or investors were of the old familiar Salon variety. One desperate solution occurred to Monet and his group; to organize an auction of their work. The event was accordingly scheduled to take place at the Paris auction rooms known as the Hôtel Drouot. The group were joined by Berthe Morisot, sister-in-law of Manet and admired by them all for her spirit and beauty.

What they needed next was

publicity. Manet volunteered to tackle the most influential, if most disliked, critic in Paris, Albert Wolff of the newspaper *Le Figaro*. Manet's letter was couched in suitably submissive terms: 'You do not as yet perhaps appreciate this kind of painting, but you will like it some day. And it would be very kind of you to mention it in *Le Figaro*.'

Wolff duly responded. Manet, after all, was the respected revolutionary who had shocked the art establishment, not to mention members of the public, with his heretical *Olympia* in 1865. He wrote: 'There may be some good business here for anyone wishing to speculate in future art.' He went on: 'But the impression that the Impressionists achieve is that of a cat walking on the keyboard of a piano, or of a monkey who has somehow got hold of a box of paints.' The friends, no doubt managing with difficulty to keep their tempers, appealed to the public, in an introduction in the catalogue, to be given a chance. They might have been encouraged to learn that their friend Durand-Ruel was to officiate on the day of the sale, as the appointed expert.

The event turned into a shambles. The auctioneer sent for the police to impose some sort of order as supporters of the artists were howled down during the bidding by a crowd

LEFT
Railway Bridge, Argenteuil, 1873

BELOW
The Pont de L'Europe,
Gare St-Lazare, 1877

"*You do not appreciate this kind of painting, but you will like it some day...*"
Edouard Manet

who had come for the fun. Durand-Ruel was unable to secure any of the group's offerings from their own studios, such was the hubbub. Constant heckling drowned the bidding, making the auctioneer's job practically impossible. Durand-Ruel watched helplessly as works were knocked down to negligible prices. He did, however, manage later to buy many of them back, including some that had found buyers only by virtue of their elegant frames. Berthe Morisot's pictures fared relatively well in the circumstances – she easily outsold Monet, Sisley and Renoir. It was remarked in a press report of the

PARIS: *the steam age*

event: 'We had some good fun with the purple landscapes, red flowers, black rivers, yellow and green women and blue children which the new School presented for the admiration of the populace.'

Monet, virtually penniless, returned to Argenteuil. He wrote to a Roumanian collector, Georges de Bellio, who had bought one of his paintings of Le Havre, offering to sell him his stock of 25 unsold paintings for five francs. The militant art scribe,

---

Albert Wolff, resumed his attack in terms redolent of a modern Fleet Street tabloid: 'Yesterday a poor soul was arrested in the street after seeing the exhibition, for biting the passers-by.' Nor was distaste for Monet and the other Impressionists confined to the illiterate. Henry James, a cultivated Bostonian man-of-letters, who liked to keep up with the arts in London and Paris, sent an article on the Impressionists to a New York paper regretting the passing of 'the good old rules which decreed that beauty is beauty and ugliness is ugliness.'

Despite all the hostility, 1876 turned out to be an encouraging year for Monet and his friends, in quality and volume of work produced if not yet in hard sales. Sisley discovered new

LEFT
La Rue Montorgueil:
la fête du 30 Juin, 1878

RIGHT
The Hôtel des Roches Noires at Trouville, 1870

themes in the flood waters of Marly. Pissarro, re-installed in Pontoise, was displaying a fresh vigour and inventiveness.

Monet, back in Argenteuil, took his *Woman with a Parasol* to Paris, where his eyes were opened by a new phenomenon, the mighty railway station, Gare Saint-Lazare. The experience of standing amid the steam and din contained within its great glass roof, the swirling vapour and ghostly figures, now concealed, now apparent, excited him as a 'realist' theme that demanded to be captured. Aesthetic considerations did not apply. What gripped Monet was the relationship, in this hissing, thundering place, between man and machine. The total experience was what challenged him to confront the subject head-on. Later, he enjoyed telling the story of how he put on his best suit, introduced himself to the station-master as 'Claude Monet the painter', and requested facilities to paint on the spot. The station-master, impressed, had the engines re-charged with coal to provide maximum drama: when Monet had finished he was bowed off the premises with appropriate ceremony.

That summer, Monet visited a wealthy client, Ernest Hoschedé, a substantial collector and owner of a department store in Paris. It was to prove a fateful association. Hoschedé was shortly declared bankrupt and was obliged to sell all his property, including his collection. Hoschedé himself disappeared. Monet, meanwhile, had decided it was time to quit Argenteuil. The rapid advance of urbanization was growing more and more depressing. The pollution was barely tolerable; the river had become a sewer. This was no sudden catastrophe: Monet had seen it coming but had continued to paint as if everything around him was as it used to be. He withdrew more and more deeply into his garden and turned his back on the town.

Between leaving Argenteuil and moving to Vétheuil, Monet spent six weeks in Paris, lodging near the Place de l'Europe. When the city put out its

flags for the national holiday - in those days, 30 June – he painted two versions of the scene, one on the rue Saint-Denis and the other on the rue Montorgueil. Both works, which were included in the Impressionist exhibition of 1874, helped to capture a new mood in the capital. Paris was *en*

fête for the first time since the Commune, the blood-stained aftermath of the Franco-Prussian War, when a total ban on public gatherings had been imposed for fear of further anti-government demonstrations. These are the first festive street scenes by Monet since his study of

SOUTH OF FRANCE: *the call of the sun*

The Hôtel des Roches Noires at Trouville three years earlier, which achieves an equally vibrant effect as bright flags snap in the seaside breeze – perhaps the last painting Monet was able to finish before the outbreak of war brought excursions of any kind to a stop.

In the spring of 1878 Camille gave birth to a second son, Michel; but the delivery left her in dangerously poor health. That summer, the Monets turned their backs on Argenteuil and moved further down the river to Vétheuil, a rural community of some 600, and out of range of the encroaching industrial squalor. Alice Hoschedé and her six children, with no roof over their heads, were grateful to be offered shelter by the Monets in their new home. It was there, a few months later, that Camille Monet died.

One of the Hoschedé sons, Jean-Pierre, was to write of Monet's visit to his parents' estate at Montgeron shortly after the crisis in his father's affairs. His recollections are from his early childhood, but they throw a wry light on the effect of that fateful future event on the lives of both families. He remembered a party at which everyone had to come with ugly made-up faces. Monet and Renoir had come adorned with repellent fake scars. A swarm of other artists, of the kind his father liked to entertain, turned up. And he particularly remembered Monet's portrait of the lovely Camille, her dress dotted with sunlight.

Ten years later Hoschedé died. Alice and Monet decided to marry. With Alice caring for the children, Monet was now free to travel. He embarked on a three-month winter painting tour to Bordighera, just over the Italian border from Menton. Here he wrote to Alice: 'It is wonderful weather and I wish I could send you a little sunshine. I am slaving away on six paintings a day...the light is really terrifying. I have already spent many sessions on some studies that I can't quite bring off. The joy is that I can return to the subject each day, knowing it is possible to do battle

with no change in effect.'

He spent the following two years revisiting his favourite haunts along the Normandy coast and the mouth of the Seine – Dieppe, Varengevilie, Etretat, Honfleur. Above all, he was delighted to renew his life-long passion for the sea. He claimed that he gained strength from sea air – it fuelled his enthusiasm for painting direct from nature and absorbing himself in his native creeks and coasts.

In the autumn of 1886 he set off on a painting expedition to Belle-Ile, off the Atlantic coast of western Brittany, where he tackled a

combination of grottoes, outcrops and needle-sharp rocks in a wild sea. Six months later, the Belle-Ile paintings were exhibited at the Georges Petit Gallery in Paris and were a great success. Later that year, by way of contrast, he visited Antibes and Juan-les-Pins on the Côte d'Azur, where he revelled in the clear pinks and blues.

One writer, Gustave Geffroy, describes a conversation with Monet when on a two-man expedition to the Creuse valley in central France, a location that provided Monet with some of his most dramatic landscapes. Typically self-critical, he complained that he was 'tracking nature without

being able to capture it.' His subject, the gloomy beauty of the two Creuses, anticipates the grandeur of his later *Rouen Cathedral* series.

Monet treated these forays into the natural world with respect. The conditions he had to contend with, it

LEFT
Antibes, 1888

TOP RIGHT
Antibes seen from Plateau
Nôtre-Dame, 1888

ABOVE
Photograph of Antibes, South of France

was remarked at the time, would deter a man half his age. They involved wearing full seaman's gear, sweater, balaclava, thick boots, windcheater; and a rugged constitution.

Reviewers of his exhibitions never ceased to marvel at his perception of natural effects, his quick analysis of the subject caught in a few apparently random strokes which emerge as flowing water, gushing torrents or hurtling spray. 'He studies the land,' marvelled one reviewer, 'like a geologist. With the tip of his brush he illuminates the very veins of a rock. He paints grass dried by the wind or drenched by the rain, or wet rock on which the sea leaves clumps of sticky weed.' Geffroy wrote: 'There are effects that have never been tried before – three straight lines, two grassy slopes whose bases intercept. Light ends up changing the nature of the objects, which become transparent as though lit from within.'

Monet's decision to move to Vétheuil, and the responsibility for providing for a much-enlarged family, did nothing to ease his basic

NORMANDY: *rainy days at Pourville*

anxiety – that of continuing to paint while selling virtually nothing. After their three years at Vétheuil, he decided they must all move to Poissy for the sake of the children's schooling. Conditions there, however, turned out to be impossible as far as Monet was concerned. They moved again, this time to the small resort of Pourville, where it rained incessantly. The entire household was flooded out. Monet wrote to Durand-Ruel that he could not even think about painting: 'We are literally under water.' In desperation he settled on a more likely haven than the sodden villages along the Seine. He told his now desperate

" With Monet, light ends up changing the very nature of objects which become transparent as though lit from within "

Gustave Geffroy

family that they were moving to a place where he could work. It was called Giverny; and he was to be there for the rest of his life.

ABOVE
Cap Martin, Near Menton, 1884

TOP RIGHT
Rapids on the Petite Creuse at Fresselines, 1889

RIGHT
Ravine of the Creuse in Sunlight, 1889

BACK ON THE SEINE

GIVERNY: *a turn of the tide* _____

The house he had found to rent, known as The Cider Press, close by the River Epte, offered enough room to house the entire family while providing Monet with a roomy studio and a barn to house his equipment. The surroundings were pleasantly rural and included remnants of two gardens and an orchard. One of their first visitors was Monet's friend and fellow painter, Caillebotte, who arrived in his boat. Suddenly the talk was all of gardening. At the same time, Monet's thoughts were turning to the river and how it could once again play a part in his work. He had somehow managed to hang on to his painting-boat, a relic of Argenteuil, which was soon moored nearby.

Monet already knew the district around Giverny. He had walked its lanes, sailed on its waters and endured the floods which had periodically swamped the family's rented homes along the river. After a one-man show at Durand-Ruel's he was looking for a fresh start. Before long he and his two young sons, plus the Hoschedés, were settled in what was to be their last home. The entire family set to work. Monet began painting again. The locals, resentful and suspicious of the newcomers' bohemian ways, took their revenge by means of minor persecutions. When Monet began painting the picturesque haystacks nearby, they knocked them over. Monet did what he could by paying them off. After a while the villagers accepted the situation and gradually left the Monets in peace.

There now emerged a new Monet, a stocky figure clad in his favourite gear, thick English tweeds, topped by a straw hat. In this new guise he entertained visitors, among them Cézanne, to whom he paid tribute as one surviving master to another. He lived surrounded by a personal collection of works by Cézanne as well as by Degas, Pissarro, Sisley, Renoir and others. A vivid recollection of this time by the American painter, Mary Cassatt, the close companion of Degas, recalls her first impression: 'Like a cut-throat with large red eyeballs standing out of his head, a fearsome pointed beard, and an excited manner of talking that rattles and creaks.'

In the autumn of 1890, he made one of his rare confessions about his work to his friend and future biographer, Gustave Geffroy. 'I am

OPPOSITE
Path in Ile Saint-Martin, Vétheuil, 1880

BELOW LEFT
Recent photograph of Monet's garden at Giverny

BELOW RIGHT
The Garden Path at Giverny, 1902

GIVERNY: *a turn in the tide*

> *"Monet is no longer a painter, but a hunter"*

Guy de Maupassant

---

grinding away,' he told him, 'bent on a series of different effects. But at this time of the year the sun goes down so quickly that I can't keep up with it. I have become a very slow worker. But the further I go the better I understand that it is essential to work hard to achieve what I am looking for – above all, the same light present all around. More than ever, what comes easily in a single stroke means nothing to me. What excites me is to set down what I feel. That, it seems to me, is the way to make progress.'

By this stage in his career, one would have thought he would be less likely to modify his manner of painting than at any time in his life. He had achieved the seemingly impossible by making his name as a landscape painter in a style which, to begin with, antagonized critics and collectors, who failed to see his work not merely as original, but in the spirit of a long line of French *plein air* painting pioneered by Corot and the Barbizon painters; all of them eagerly collected by later generations. Monet now contemplated a change of subject matter; a new intensity of vision which would occupy him for the next decade. To outward appearances, he was settling into a new role. Guy de Maupassant, who had met Monet in Etretat, recalled him as 'no longer a painter but a hunter'. He described

ABOVE
Haystacks in the Snow, 1891

TOP RIGHT
Haystacks, 1891

BELOW RIGHT
Haystacks at Noon, 1891

him being followed by children who carried his canvases, five or six of which would be of the same subject painted at different times of the day and with different effects. According to Maupassant, he would lie in wait for the sun and shadows – hence the 'hunter' reference – so as to capture in a few strokes the effect of light on a passing cloud. He had seen Monet, he said, 'seize a glittering shower of light on a white cliff and fix it with a

GIVERNY: *a turn of the tide*

ABOVE
Poplars on the Epte, 1891

RIGHT
Poplars, 1891

flood of yellow tones.'

His growing fame in the United States, where Durand-Ruel had lately mounted the first-ever Impressionist exhibition across the Atlantic, began to draw American admirers and – less welcome – socialites, to his increasingly famous retreat. Monet, alternately stimulated and enraged,

turned his eye to the more fugitive aspects of Nature, forever seeking familiar subjects: misty sunshine, natural forms veiled in transient light. His fortunes continued to improve. An exhibition of his latest work sold out at impressively high prices. Pissarro wrote to his son, Lucien, in London: 'People want nothing but

Monets. It seems he can't paint enough to meet the demand. It is always the same story – everything he does goes to America at prices up to 6,000 francs.'

Monet's break-through into a seemingly magical form of Abstraction set him on the way to tackling an equally elusive subject in the same mode. His subject-matter was close at hand in rural France. For more than a decade he had painted along the Seine, where he had found enough subjects to satisfy most painters for a lifetime; but he had exhausted them by repetition. Now, in his fifties, they seemed to him insubstantial. He was ready for something more energizing, a new experience against which to brace his creative faculties, a fuel for his reawakened ambition. In 1891, he exhibited at Durand-Ruel's gallery in Paris a series, or suite, of 15 paintings of haystacks that had been standing in a field close to his home at Giverny. These could hardly have emphasized

GIVERNY: *birth of the Series paintings*

his change of direction more vividly. At first, as he explained, he had envisaged only two works, one in cloudy weather and the other in sunshine, painted in wholly different lights. He had discovered that the nature of light is that it changes continually; so he decided to record the succession of each of its different effects on a whole series of paintings, working on each in turn, each canvas being devoted to one specific effect. By ceasing work the instant the light changed, Monet achieved, in his own words, 'instantaneity'. As he suspended operations on one haystack, he would pass to another, then another, so that each individual became endowed with a specific effect as a few moments in time were captured. It was spontaneity he was after, he explained, not a composite and painterly effect. These lucent forms were in sharp contrast to his early images of creeping industrialization along the Seine.

The oft-quoted reaction of one young painter, Wassily Kandinsky, to these images, the now famous *Haystacks,* is typical of the impact they made on the walls of Durand-Ruel's gallery. 'Previously,' Kandinsky recalled, 'I knew only realistic art. Suddenly, for the first time, I saw a picture which the catalogue informed me was a haystack. I could not recognize it. I had a sense that the object in the picture was missing. What was absolutely clear to me was the unexpected power of the palette. Painting took on a fabulous strength and splendour.' That these paintings were the work of an established artist, 48 years old, must have seemed more astonishing still. Unless he knew of the Impressionists, he might have assumed *Haystacks* to be a one-off, unrelated to any art movement of that time.

By the time Monet was abandoning his old painting grounds, his reputation as a leading member of a controversial brotherhood of modern painters had rather ceased to be of much interest. Other members of the movement were going their own way. Renoir had virtually abandoned

Impressionism and was returning to classical nude forms. Pissarro, most loyal to the original aims and beliefs, no longer worked in the open air but from the window of a tall apartment block in the centre of Paris. Cézanne found everything he needed in his native homeland of Provence, absorbed in studies of Mont Sainte-Victoire. Manet, his reputation secure and a *Légion d'honneur* to show for it, was terminally ill. Degas was working on his vivid statuettes. Sisley was struggling on, weakened by poverty and neglect. The Impressionist movement was being infiltrated by 'Pointillists'. Monet himself, though devoted to his old comrades,

---

"People want nothing but Monets – he can't paint enough to meet the demand"

Camille Pissarro

---

complained; 'Our little temple has become a dull schoolroom.'

He had certainly not given up *plein air* painting. The Normandy coast still produced subjects for him. Over the next few years he made excursions to Le Havre, Etretat and Rouen, as well as a short trip to Genoa and the Côte d'Azur in company with Renoir. Such modest travels were among the few that the Impressionists now allowed themselves. Their cultural headquarters was Paris, and it was there that, like Monet, they did most of their business. A map showing their favourite painting-grounds would indicate that Paris was their centre and the Seine their route to the varied scenery and townships along its serpentine route from Honfleur to the cluster of small townships north of Paris – Vernon, Pontoise, Moisson, Argenteuil, Vétheuil, Poissy,

Bougival, Marly and Louveciennes.

In the Impressionists' time, the railway system was advancing at a great rate, giving birth to new suburbs. With such a facility on hand it is natural that a professional artist would take the most convenient route to the least expensive destinations. If there is an absence of conventionally romantic locations in their work, it could be attributed to their reluctance to move far from their homes. We see nothing in Monet's work, for example, of the Pyrenees or the Haute Savoie. Most of the Impressionists, Monet included, had a personal attachment to their birthplaces and painted best where their affections lay.

Life in the Monet household kept every member fully occupied. He had never been more productive. There was a new mastery in the movement of his brush, a delicacy in his handling of the stroke. He had no need of a preliminary drawing – the colours flowed seemingly unbidden from his fingers. In Paris, Pissarro remarked wryly that his old friend's success was harming the sales of the rest of them. 'People want nothing but Monets,' he said. 'He can't paint enough pictures to meet the demand.' There was a general feeling that *Haystacks* had become a unique symbol of the countryside and the valuable part it plays in offering mankind – not solely artists – a source of beauty and spiritual renewal.

The *Poplars* series that followed in the summer of 1891 came about as a result of a dispute between Monet and some of his neighbours who insisted that they cut these trees down for timber. They had been planted in the nearby village of Limetz, on common land a couple of miles from Giverny, along the banks of the Epte. Monet protested, but to no avail. He then decided, in partnership with a local timber merchant, to make an offer for them. Their bid was successful; thus one small corner of rural France came to be immortalized in paint. To Monet, as he boated along the river, the pattern of the poplars appeared to form its own natural composition which varied as he moved through the water. As he strove to catch exactly the right light, setting one rank of the slender trees against the other, he found himself becoming less and less aware of them as individual subjects, which was his initial intention, and more as decorative elements, interacting one with another in the elusively changing light. His *Poplars* was a manifestation of a new element of Abstraction creeping into Monet's work and taking him unawares.

In a break with convention he decided to exhibit *Poplars* alone. Hung as a group at Durand-Ruel's, and to cries of admiration from the critics, they all found buyers. Perceived as belonging to the avant-garde, he had nevertheless made 'decorative art' acceptable.

LEFT
Photograph of Rouen Cathedral, Normandy, France

BELOW LEFT
Rouen Cathedral, Midday, 1894

BELOW RIGHT
Rouen Cathedral, Evening, 1894

ROUEN: 'stones of flesh and blood'

The Rouen Cathedral series, which occupied him from 1892 to 1894 was to involve Monet in a certain amount of acrimony, as well as discomfort. Just as he was getting started at the milliner's shop in which an upstairs window was to be his vantage point, the customers began to complain of a masculine presence as they tried on hats and exchanged gossip. Monet solved the problem by building himself a relatively comfortable hutch in which he huddled in total privacy, out of sight and sound of the affronted ladies.

Some idea of the strain of Monet's self-imposed workload can be glimpsed in a note written to his wife Alice. 'Every day I add something and catch something by surprise which I had not previously been aware of,' he

LEFT
Rouen Cathedral, West Façade, Sunlight, 1894

RIGHT
Rouen Cathedral, the Façade in Sunlight, 1894

"*The artist has shown us as many subtle differences as there might be moments in a man's life*"

Georges Clemenceau

---

told her. 'It is terribly difficult, but just give me a few more days of fine weather... I had nightmares all night – the Cathedral was tumbling on top of me, all blue and pink and yellow.'

Monet and his friends always maintained that they could never be accused of glorifying the past, even to the extent of omitting such hallowed monuments as chapels and churches from their work. Consequently, his *Rouen Cathedral* series was not intended to be seen in a devotional sense, as an act of praise to the Creator. Monet was aiming at a sequence of paintings, a study of the ancient stones which he would animate simply as objects, curious but dispassionate. According to the time of day, the huge façade blushes or glows with light. Taken in sequence, it assumes a character as expressive as a series of portraits. The passing of the hours from dawn to dusk reveals it in all its different aspects until metaphorically it closes its eyes as the long day fades, the subtle and mysterious colours vanishing until the next sunrise.

Monet's paintings of the Cathedral, all viewed from the same position, number not less than 30. His interest lay not in the architecture but in the atmospheric variations which occurred throughout the course of the day.

To Monet, the Cathedral was in a constant state of flux, as light and shadow, tint and form, passed before his eyes. Once finished, he hesitated before exhibiting the series, but a number were eventually shown by Durand-Ruel two years later. Monet's friend, Georges Clemenceau wrote an article about them in terms which pleased Monet: 'The artist has shown us in these 20 canvases, each subtly

different in its effect, what he would have felt had he done 50, 100, or 1,000 such paintings, as many as there might be moments in a man's life – supposing his life could last as long as this monument of stone.' The *Cathedral* series, in five versions, each with its individual colour harmony, is represented in the Musée d'Orsay – a celebration of Monet's status as the great creative artist of his day. Because it was intended to be seen as a total experience, no one painting is quite complete without the others. Some of the critics of the time were offended that such liberties had been taken with the revered medieval monument and that such a masterpiece of Gothic architecture should have been adopted as a motif by a mere artist. Another critic found

ABOVE
The Seine at Giverny, 1897

BELOW
The Seine at Giverny,
Morning Mists, 1895

ROUEN: *'the one reality is light'*

RIGHT
A field of poppies photographed in France

BELOW
Poppy Field in a Hollow Near Giverny,
1885

FAR RIGHT
Rain, Etretat, 1886

the series poetic: 'After centuries of embodying the mystical aspirations of the multitudes, the stones have become human,' he wrote. 'They have become flesh and blood.'

It was in Monet's nature to view with caution the increasing enthusiasm with which, as he grew older, each of his new works was received. He told Geffroy that the further he advanced, the harder he found it to convey what he felt. 'Anyone who claims he has finished a work has to be terribly arrogant. To finish means to complete, but I am forcing myself to work without making much progress.' In a letter to his ever-patient Alice, he confessed that 'this cursed Cathedral' was hard work. He told her that since starting a week ago he had worked without a break, yet still he could not achieve the effect he was after. 'It will come in the end,' he told her, 'but not without hard struggle.' In such flashes of candour towards those closest to him he was able to relieve his feelings while preserving his public reputation. He could tell Alice how 'ghastly' the job was as a means of giving vent to his doubts and frustrations: this was the personal price he paid for the creative process. Monet never pretended that producing a work of art, especially on a grand scale, was anything other than 'a kind of pain'.

In a project prompted by a nostalgia of sorts, Monet next embarked on a series of works, *Morning on the Seine*, which occupied him throughout the autumn of 1895 in which he was to probe even deeper into the nature of light. The evidence suggests that he painted from a flat-bottomed boat, a device he was well used to, and that he started work virtually at daybreak. In this way he was able to follow the course of the sun as it slowly invaded the scene. His friend Geffroy wrote: 'What does the subject matter? What does the landscape matter that Monet is trying to paint? He knows that there is only one reality and that is light. Without it everything would be shrouded in chaotic night. It is light that is all-powerful, that magnifies forms and

brings out their beauty.' Another critic called him France's greatest painter. 'He knows all that is beautiful in our countryside – red pine trees against a blue sky, the contours of cliffs effaced by fog, water running under fresh foliage.'

Monet's paintings of the cliff-tops of his native Normandy, with their subtle changes of form and colour, their endless conflict with the sea, are full of his characteristic verve and spirit. In 1896, he began a series of watercolour studies, a medium which he appears to have found less demanding for his present purpose. Out on the cliff-top, at a time in his career when he was no longer desperate to make his mark, he would have particularly enjoyed revisiting

---

"He knows that there is only one reality, and that is light"

Gustave Geffroy

---

the scenes of his boyhood. The character of the *Cliffs* paintings has much in common with other work in which he had recently been engaged. It was atmospheric and poetical; floating pinks and greys, sea-greens and lyrical blues. He found it hard work, and the wind and cold slowed him down. His tendency towards Abstraction, noticeable in the *Rouen Cathedral* series, lends an ethereal air to these cliff-top paintings, as if the rocks and buildings – some of them Napoleonic look-out posts along the coast – were hardly less material than the atmosphere that envelops them.

The sea, in a sense, was Monet's natural element. Ever since his schooldays it had drawn him back, re-awakening old sensations and producing new ones. In some of these late *Cliffs* paintings he achieves a similar vibrance and abstraction to that of *Haystacks*: material forms dissolving in variegated light.

His readiness to tackle Nature face-to-face became legendary. One of the most famous examples, chronicled by Monet himself, is of an incident at Etretat that could very well have

LONDON *and the Thames* _____

ended in disaster. As he himself told the story, he was hoping for a good day's painting at Etretat, hard at work beneath the famous cliff in a high wind and with the rough sea crashing about him, safely protected – as he thought – against the tide, which he assumed was on the ebb even if waves seemed to be lapping round his feet. Absorbed as he was, he failed to see a huge wave coming, which swept him up bodily against the cliff face along with all his painting gear. As it receded, the wave dragged him down, momentarily submerged him, and left him to scramble back on all fours. His boots, thick stockings and top-coat were soaked through. The palette which he had been holding had become smeared all over his face, covering his beard in blue and yellow. He completely lost the painting he had been working on, along with his easel and rucksack. When he had

TOP LEFT
London, Parliament with the Sun Breaking Through the Fog, 1904

BELOW LEFT
Waterloo Bridge, London, At Dusk, 1903

ABOVE
London, Houses of Parliament, 1905

RIGHT
River Thames and the Houses of Parliament, London, as they are today

"*The Thames was all gold and gleamingly beautiful* "

Claude Monet

LONDON: *vistas from the Savoy*

recovered and dried himself he was enraged to find that he could not work; the subject he had been counting on was no longer there. He immediately dashed off a telegram ordering replacements for everything he had lost. The work was still to be done, and Monet was not finished yet.

Though Monet was not particularly fond of travelling abroad, he seems to have had a soft spot for London. Despite the anxiety of his first visit as a refugee from the Prussians, he had not wasted his time there. The companionship of Pissarro and Daubigny, and the fruitful association with Durand-Ruel, had been of great value to him. If he found little in the painting there to sharpen his appetite, he at least become acquainted with the far more appealing work of those English masters of landscape, Turner and Constable. In 1891 he once more crossed the Channel, after receiving an invitation to exhibit at the new English Art Club, and again in 1898 to visit his son Michel, whom he had sent there to learn English.

Whether he was encouraged by his womenfolk, or simply by a desire to revisit the scenes he had painted during his voluntary exile, Monet returned to London, accompanied by Alice and Suzanne, in September 1899. This time there was no problem about accommodation – they moved into the Savoy Hotel. Apart from its obvious amenities, the Savoy occupies a site overlooking the Thames, with vistas of two bridges not far from the Houses of Parliament. It was to provide ample inspiration for a painter of such imaginative power as Monet.

The Thames Below Westminster, 1871

FROM LONDON TO THE SUN _____

He returned home with close on 40 new works, which he exhibited in 1904. The subjects included Charing Cross Bridge, Waterloo Bridge and the Houses of Parliament – the most extensive series of London scenes by any major artist of his time.

Without the fog, Monet declared later, London would not be the beautiful city it was. What to most Londoners might have seemed grimly Dickensian struck him as a fantastic canopy of glistening vapour, mother-of-pearl highlights and mysterious glowing colours.

He was to recall with pleasure the factory chimneys, terraced houses and luminous fogs that settled on the city day by day. The sight of the Thames from London's bridges enraptured him; the reflected street-lights wavering in its mysterious depths and stone monuments and statues hovering like ghosts.

ABOVE
Charing Cross Bridge, c.1903

TOP RIGHT
The Doge's Palace in Venice, 1908

RIGHT
Photograph of the Doge's Palace, Venice, Italy

He saw colour everywhere, as if at a fairground seen through drizzle and mist. To a visiting poet and art scholar, Gustave Kahn, who was in town to cover an exhibition of Monet's works for the *Gazette des Beaux Arts,* they resembled a great green forest woven in a violet mist. These grand architectural subjects are on a scale never envisaged by earlier masters. Their grandeur is all the more impressive for the absence of context – a situation or neighbourhood which would give us a sense of scale. Each

work is a response to a closely observed atmospheric effect, drenched in light and atmosphere – as one critic put it, 'sensation transformed into reverie.' Wherever they are shown, their presence is a reminder that, to Monet, nothing that his eye lit upon was ever perfectly still.

It could be that Monet's success with his London series encouraged him to think of his subsequent works in similar terms. The impact and cohesion of his later series, from *Haystacks* onwards, owe much to his London experience. It was fortunate for the English that one of the greatest of modern painters should have had a soft spot for the Thames. Monet's tourism took him to the Tower of London and other historic monuments, and he was among the throng who stood in the streets bare-headed at Queen Victoria's funeral. It was in London, too, that he acquired a

"*Venice is very beautiful and I am sad I shall soon have to leave this unique light. What a shame I didn't come here as a younger man, when I was full of daring...*"

Claude Monet

VENICE: *a crowning jewel*

taste for the English breakfast, and for English tweeds, which were to remain his standard garb for the rest of his life.

He would have found in the London of the 1890s a more congenial political climate than that which prevailed in his own country at that time, poisoned as it was by the

ABOVE
The Grand Canal, Venice, 1908

RIGHT
Photographic view of the Grand Canal, Venice, Italy

FAR RIGHT
Monet painting in his studio

Dreyfus scandal and the consequent outburst of anti-semitism. Pissarro, himself a Jew, wrote to his son Lucien early in 1898 that he was right to stay in England where he could expect 'more justice and tolerance,' adding: 'Here I fear, the end has come.' In London, Monet renewed his friendship with Whistler, whom he had known in Paris and whose American origins had not prevented him from becoming the darling of the literary and artistic salons, or from receiving from the French the coveted *Légion d'honneur*. There was a certain affinity between the two painters, perhaps recognized only by themselves; their sensitive handling of the murky beauty of a river veiled in bluish light.

When Monet's London paintings were exhibited at Durand-Ruel's gallery in 1904 they were an immediate success. There was praise for the way he had managed to give form and substance to subjects so ephemeral and elusive. One critic ventured to make a direct comparison between Monet and Turner. To compare the two, he suggested, side by side on a gallery wall, would unite two examples of exceptional visual sensitivity. Delighted by this reception, Monet had thoughts of mounting a similar exhibition in London itself, and started to make enquiries. In the end he thought better of it, partly because Durand-Ruel had already shown many of the London paintings in his Bond Street gallery. He had no need of the money. It was time to turn his thoughts to other things.

Monet's attention now turned to another of Europe's architectural masterpieces – the city of Venice. He had lately received an invitation to paint there and become part of a tradition that had stretched from Canaletto to Turner. This illustrious connection understandably appealed to him. He was nearly 70, at an age when most painters would be thought unlikely to respond to new challenges. Monet set off, was moved by what he saw, painted with his usual zest, and went back for a second trip the

GIVERNY: *epic poems of nature*

following year. The results were typically his own; no regard was paid to how other artists had portrayed the city over the centuries. Regardless of the function of these buildings, whether religious or otherwise, he turned his dispassionate eye on each one he painted and transformed it into a miracle of reflections and light. Monet wrote home: 'What a pity I did not come here when I was young and bold and would stop at nothing! No matter – I am spending delicious moments here, almost forgetting I am an old man.'

By now his celebrity had reached new heights. He was 'the epic poet of Nature', wrote one admirer, 'extracting from Nature all its joy, one

ABOVE
Monet in his garden at Giverny

LEFT
Monet in his studio at Giverny

of the crowning jewels of our epoch.' In a review of his next exhibition at Durand-Ruel's, one French critic declared that Monet's work was, above all, the expression of the essential France. 'He is our greatest landscape painter.'

" A private domain of astonishing beauty, lovingly supervised by its creator... "

Claude Monet

The origins of Monet's last series, his waterlily sequence, lie in his creation of one of the world's most beautiful gardens, at Giverny, his journey's end. This urge to create a garden was stimulated by his life-long fascination with water and an increasing interest in horticulture. Together these prompted him to create a garden devoted to the cultivation of exotic species of waterlilies and other aquatic plants.

After several years of careful cultivation, the water garden developed into a private domain of astonishing beauty, lovingly supervised by its creator.

In February 1893, Monet had bought a piece of land directly opposite his house. This new plot was separated from the main property by a small, winding road, and by a single railway track connecting Vernon with Gisors. The property was crossed by a swiftly-flowing communal stream, the Ru, which had been created by monks in the middle ages for breeding fish. The plot included a small pond, probably formed when the river was diverted to allow a way through for the new railway track. Already growing on the pond was the common, hardy white species of waterlily.

Monet managed to buy this patch of land as an extension to his flower garden, which was slowly taking shape across the road. He made two immediate additions to the pond. First, to provide ideal growing

ABOVE
Monet's house at Giverny

LEFT
The garden at Giverny today

GIVERNY: *a world of waterlilies*

conditions for the more exotic species of waterlily, he constructed two sluices at the eastern and western ends of the pond. When these were closed they ensured a perfectly still surface, enabling the temperature of the water to rise as it was warmed by the sun. When the sluices were opened the river was channelled into the pond, providing a source of fresh water. As a finishing touch, Monet had an arched bridge built over the pond, inspired

by his collection of Japanese prints. The bridge and its reflections transformed the pond into an *al fresco* work of art.

Monet's paintings of this first water garden, dating from winter to the early spring of 1895, were followed by a second series four years later. By this time the garden itself had reached new heights of splendour, as his paintings of it reveal. With the urge to extend still further, he bought more

land adjacent to the garden, and applied for permission to divert the little river to water it. This time the locals insisted on a civil investigation. But Monet had his way. The river flowed into its new bed with no loss to the villagers, and the magical garden blossomed anew.

The 'Japanese' bridge, the luxuriant blossoms, and their reflections in the clear pool, delighted Monet. As he grew older he was relieved that he was no longer forced to travel in search of new subjects to paint; all he needed was here, before his very eyes. The garden became a theme that continued to engross him for the rest of his life, a poetic ensemble of waterlilies silently gliding; willows rising above, their branches softly cascading: and the ever-changing light, colours in the clouds, mirrored in the reflecting calm.

"With the Waterlilies *M. Monet becomes an artist of the 20th century"*

Le Journal

GIVERNY: *floral seas and mists*

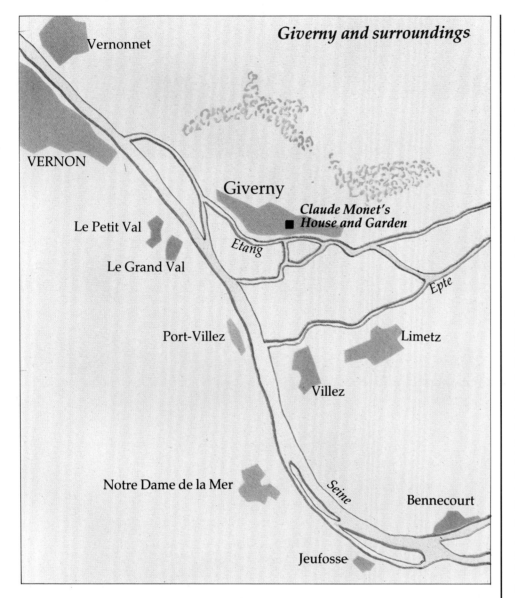

Giverny and surroundings

Vernonnet

VERNON

Giverny

■ *Claude Monet's House and Garden*

Etang

Le Petit Val

Le Grand Val

Epte

Port-Villez

Limetz

Villez

Notre Dame de la Mer

Seine

Bennecourt

Jeufosse

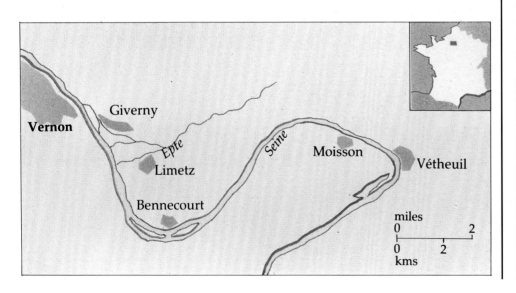

Vernon

Giverny

Epte

Seine

Limetz

Moisson

Vétheuil

Bennecourt

miles
0   2
0   2
kms

Julie Manet, daughter of the painter, on a visit to the house and garden, noted in her diary that Monet had made himself a white-decorated bedroom above the studio with large windows. Her feminine eye also noted that Alice's bedroom had blue panelling, and those of her eldest daughters, were in mauve. The drawing-room, panelled in violet, was hung with Japanese prints. She and her cousin Jeanne were shown the garden and the Japanese bridge before being taken to the station to take the train home. Julie thought it must be 'quite delightful' to have your own country house and be able to see it from time to time from the train, appearing like a shadow in the night, and say to oneself, 'it's mine.'

Today, Monet's garden at Giverny, fully restored and visited by thousands, must rank as his most enduring masterpiece – enduring in the sense that it in a constant state of renewal and replenishment by nature;

Towards Giverny

Monet continued to live and paint along the Seine producing a steady flow of work to culminate in the *Haystacks* series, paintings of poplars along the Epte and the magical *Nymphéas* inspired by his garden at Giverny

a masterpiece because it is unique and cannot be repeated. It was the inspiration for some of Monet's last and most magical paintings, the *Nymphéas*.

The house and garden were eventually bequeathed by Monet's only surviving son to the Marmottan, part of the Académie des Beaux Arts, with a stipulation that no more than six people could visit the house in any one week. When Michel Monet died in 1966, leaving all the paintings to the Musée Marmottan, they had the choice of either building a gallery in Paris or using the existing ones at Giverny. The idea of reconstructing the whole complex was only realized in recent times.

Claude Monet had insisted that three heated greenhouses should be devoted to exotic plants and orchids. One already contained a small pool in which waterlilies flowered in the

GIVERNY: *a painting in itself*

winter. There was a special room beneath the second greenhouse where tulip bulbs were stored, sorted by colour, for planting in autumn. His intention was that the flowers should be seen in blocks of colour – floral seas and mists – and no one was allowed to pick them. The second garden was in effect the waterlily pond, and one gardener was employed full-time to tend it. The third garden was for raising bedding-out plants, enabling him to reserve his other gardens for purely decorative display.

Monet's working methods fascinated visitors to Giverny. A painter friend of the Impressionists' circle, Georges Jeanniot, watching him at work, remarked on the way he attacked the blank canvas, having first brushed in a few lines in charcoal, handling his long brushes with deft, sure strokes in sessions lasting about an hour. His step-son, Jean-Pierre Hoschedé, vowed that he had never heard Monet use the word 'finished', that he never signed his paintings in advance of delivering them to a gallery, and that he tended to leave unpainted patches around the edges, to be filled in when the time came for him to add his signature – often with reluctance, since he regarded his first impressions as more valid than the 'finished' ones. His studio was stocked with such works which Monet could not bear to let go.

The basic element of the *Nymphéas* paintings, he explained, is 'the mirror of water which constantly changes as fragments of reflection from the sky flicker on the surface, giving it light and movement.' A passing cloud, a fresh breeze, a sudden gust of wind, all contributed colour changes unnoticed by anyone but the painter, breaking up from time to time in imperceptible ripples that creased the surface, creating an expanse like watered silk. To make anything at all out of this constant change, Monet said, he needed to have five or six canvases to work on at the same time, moving from one to the other as the light-effects fluctuated and altered.

At this point, however, calamity struck when Monet began to notice that his sense of colour was beginning to fail. Reds began to look muddy, pinks paler, and the deeper tones he could not manage at all. His work was beginning to look, in his own terms, increasingly old-fashioned. The cause was a cataract. This meant painful surgery and enforced rest for six months. As his sight returned, his vision of the sky, the water and the flowers that nodded and swayed in his garden, slowly reached a semblance of normality and he began work on the ambitious plan which was still very much in the forefront of his mind. This was to create a huge new studio, 25 by 15 metres, with solid walls, only one door, and a roof composed of two-thirds glass. This took six months during which time Monet directed operations with the help of a local craftsman, who, he said, really knew his job. It was finished in the spring of 1916.

Over the next few years, while the carnage of the Great War raged in the background, Monet began to pick up the pieces of his own life and art. The waterlilies project was now begun in earnest. Views of the water from varying heights and viewpoints offered inexhaustible subject matter, ranging from depths shimmering in half-veiled light to reflections of weeping willows casting their ever-changing patterns. 'How was it possible?' asked a visitor. 'Don't bother your head about that,' Monet told him. 'It is because I have adapted my working methods to my eyesight.'

To Monet, the waterlily pool was a painting in itself. He thought of it in those terms, and integral to the spirit of Impressionist invention. As he progressed, the Japanese bridge was gradually assuming less importance, allowing the water to occupy the whole canvas. The theme became an obsession, testing Monet's imaginative powers and physical health to the limit. 'I am an old man,' he wrote to Geffroy. 'I know it is beyond my strength but I do need to set down what I experience.'

Monet's fascination with the pool, the light effects that turned it into a living canvas, its arresting beauty that varied from minute to minute, absorbed him for the rest of his life – a magical scene belonging to the natural world but at the same time of his own making. As with *Haystacks, Poplars,* and *Rouen Cathedral,* surfaces were bathed in light that changed, dissolved and re-formed from one minute to another. In an effort to catch his subject in all its moods, Monet worked with large brushes, pushing the pigment about, discovering new motifs as he did so, overpainting as surfaces shifted, bringing colours into ever more vivid juxtaposition.

The effects he achieved towards the end are among the most wonderfully ethereal of his career, anticipating Abstraction in its purest forms. In such moments Monet was painting more instinctively, unconscious perhaps, that he was even doing so. 'I forget altogether the most elementary rules of painting – if any such things exist,' he wrote to Durand-Ruel, adding wryly, 'though I know that, just the same, they will be a great success.'

When a journalist who had successfully penetrated Monet's lair in the summer of 1888 asked to be shown his studio, Monet replied by waving an arm to encompass the surrounding countryside. 'That is my studio,' he said. Invited to step inside, the visitor was shown a bed, a chest-of-drawers, a wall-cupboard, a table with some books on it, and hanging on every wall the unmistakable works of the master himself. Such was his urgent enthusiasm when seized with a particular idea, that Blanche Hoschedé, his step-daughter, would fill a wheelbarrow with canvases and follow him over fields, knowing full well that he would call for a fresh one when any sudden variation of light occurred. It was said that in London, in his favourite room in the Savoy Hotel, he was always surrounded by up to 100 canvases already prepared in advance.

His feeling for colour, much admired by his fellow painters, kept him in a state of perpetual excitement in which he would snatch one canvas

ABOVE
Waterlilies, c.1914-17

after another in an effort to record some new angle of perception. This could lead to a certain lack of 'finish' which exasperated even the patient

Durand-Ruel in the firing-line of clients' complaints that Monet did not seem always to be giving them their money's worth. His 'series' paintings were always seen to best advantage as a group, as Monet originally intended, most notably his *Poplars on the Epte* and the highly popular *Haystacks*. Monet himself, compulsive and self-critical, at one time feared that he might be turning into a 'painting machine'. Yet there is nothing mechanical in the series paintings: quite the reverse. His art was not of a kind which sought to reproduce images faithfully as a photographer might, but to spark a reaction in the viewer that would be as spiritually uplifting as a snatch of poetry or a few bars of well-loved music.

In 1891, Monet helped organize a retrospective exhibition in Paris, including a number of works from his pre-Impressionist years. His exhibitions in Boston, USA, were likewise very successful. Thanks to numerous bequests by local citizens in later years, the Museum of Fine Arts now has the largest collection of his work outside France. He campaigned to ensure that Manet's *Olympia*, one of the seminal artworks of the century, went to the Louvre. His own late paintings, which have come to be seen as owing little to Impressionism as such, revived some of the professional resentment that followed him as his fortunes improved. As he grew older he exploited his name and reputation to good effect, which included persuading a deeply unsympathetic Louvre to accept his friend Caillebotte's superb collection of early Impressionist paintings.

He never tired of telling the story of his early days in Normandy, when Boudin was his mentor and master. He recalled that he had charged between 10 and 20 francs for those early works produced under Boudin's eye, and that he had signed himself with his second name, Oscar. He considered that his first sketching expeditions with Boudin had taught him an understanding of Nature and to love it with a lasting passion. He credited Corot and Jongkind with

GIVERNY: *a fading of the light* _____

being the true founders of Impressionism. In retrospect, he even acknowledged that his spell in North Africa, as a teenage conscript, had not been wasted. Algeria, he said, 'entranced' him. There had been a fellow Norman in the ranks with whom he had much in common, and who had held on to numerous drawings and watercolours that Monet had left behind when he had been invalided out while still in his teens. Above all, Monet liked to tell people, it was in Algeria that he discovered 'the instantaneity of light'.

A description by Théodore Duret of Monet at work conveys something of his painterly technique and frame of mind. 'We must accompany him into the fields and face being burnt by the sun or stand with him knee-deep in snow. He proceeds to cover the virgin surface of his canvas with carefully placed patches of colour. This might be followed next day with attention to key details of the subject, until it begins to emerge in specific detail, catching any passing effect. On a sunny day the play of light, the tones of clouds, determine what he sees and feels.' A critic invited to the opening of an exhibition of his latest landscapes recorded Monet's words after the opening. 'No one laughed in front of my paintings.' The experience of that first humiliating Impressionist exhibition at the outset of his career was never forgotten.

For Monet in old age, the masterpiece he had created at Giverny was the climax of a life that had begun in poverty and drama, followed by disappointment and neglect. He continued to use the term 'Impressionism', though not in connection with his own work. He would describe his water garden as a living palette, with water as the basic

creative element, its appearance fluctuating as fragments of shifting light, reflections of sky and clouds, created a constant state of change. At 80 years old, reported a literary journalist who visited the Cider Press to interview him, Monet looked 20 years younger. Not that Monet gave any thought to such matters: he was as obsessed as ever with his quest, which showed no signs of diminishing.

One day, a visitor was startled to see thick smoke pouring from a bonfire in Monet's garden. He was feeding it with paintings. Their ashes glowed in heaps. Monet explained that he was remembering Manet, after whose death dealers had rushed to lay hands on all the works he had left behind, even the smallest sketches. 'I got worried,' Monet said, 'so I decided I would destroy everything that I didn't like before the dealers could grab it.' He had lately written to his distinguished old friend, Georges Clemenceau, one of Europe's foremost statesmen, that he was recovering his taste for food and also sleeping better, thanks to his two devoted doctors. He had even been taking up his palette and brushes again. Meanwhile, he was occupying himself with new projects for his garden and studio. 'So, with courage, I am getting the upper hand.'

Courage was not enough. At midday on 5 December 1926, Claude Monet died. Clemenceau, who had arrived in time, closed his old friend's eyes. Monet had let it be known that he wanted only the simplest of funeral services. Following local custom, his body was borne to the graveyard on the old cart that served as a hearse, followed by a cortège of family and a handful of friends.

Waterlilies, 1917

INDEX

Page numbers in italics refer to illustrations